Name _____ Date _____

More, Fewer, and Same

Match.

Circle the set that has fewer.

1.

Match.

Circle the set that has more.

2.

Test Prep

3. Fill in the ○ for the correct answer.

Find the set with more.

○   ○

Explain how you know which set has more in item 2.

_____

_____

Use with text pages 7–8.

1

Numbers 0 Through 9

Count. Write the number.

1.   _ _ _ _ _ _ _ _ _ _
   four

2.   _ _ _ _ _ _ _ _ _ _
   six

3. _ _ _ _ _ _ _ _ _ _
   two

4. _ _ _ _ _ _ _ _ _ _
   nine

5. _ _ _ _ _ _ _ _ _ _
   seven

6. _ _ _ _ _ _ _ _ _ _
   eight

Test Prep

Fill in the ○ for the correct answer. NH means Not Here.
How many shapes are there?

7.

five	four	three	NH
○	○	○	○

8.

0	6	10	NH
○	○	○	○

Explain how you knew the correct answer.

_____

_____

Use with text pages 9–12.

Numbers 10 Through 20

Count. Write the number.

1.
15

fifteen

2.

_____

nineteen

3.

eleven

Test Prep

Fill in the ○ for the correct answer. NH means Not Here.
How many dots are there?

4.

13   15   17   NH
○   ○   ○   ○

5.

eighteen seventeen sixteen NH
○   ○   ○   ○

Use with text pages 13–16.

Order

Write the numbers. Use the number lines.

1. Just before

, 7, 8

☐, 14, 15

2. Just after

9, 10, ☐

17, 18, ☐

3. Between

15, ☐, 17

17, ☐, 19

4. Just before and just after

☐, 2, ☐

☐, 12, ☐

Test Prep

Fill in the ○ for the correct answer. NH means Not Here.
Which number is missing?

5. 10, 11, 12, ☐

12   13   14   NH
○   ○   ○   ○

6. ☐, 18, 19, 20

15   16   17   NH
○   ○   ○   ○

Explain how you knew which number to fill in.

_____

_____

Use with text pages 17–18.

Comparing Numbers

Count.

Write the numbers that make the sentence true.

1.

___10___ is less than _____.

2.

_____ is greater than _____.

3.

_____ is greater than _____.

4.

_____ is equal to _____.

Test Prep

Fill in the ○ for the correct answer. NH means Not Here.

5. Which number is greater
   than 12?

   7   10   14   NH
   ○   ○   ○   ○

6. Which number is less than
   10?

   18   11   15   NH
   ○   ○   ○   ○

Explain how you knew which number to fill in.

_____

_____

Use with text pages 21–22.

Name _____ Date _____

Greater Than, Less Than

Use the number lines.
Circle the greater number.

1. 12   (15)   2. 18   8   3. 0   1

Use the number lines.
Circle the lesser number.

4. 7   11   5. 13   14   6. 6   7

Test Prep

7. Fill in the ○ for the correct answer. NH means Not Here.
   Which set is true?

less than 8   greater than 7   less than 3   NH
   ○   ○   ○   ○

Use with text pages 23–24.

Name _____ Date _____

Problem Solving:
Draw a Picture

1. Marisa has 9 marbles.
   Jean has 1 more.
   How many marbles does
   Jean have?

   Jean has ___10___ marbles.

Draw or write to explain.

2. Ellen has 11 coins.
   She has 7 pennies.
   She also has dimes.
   How many dimes does
   she have?

   Ellen has _____ dimes.

Test Prep

3. Fill in the ○ for the correct answer. NH means Not Here.

   There are 9 rabbits.
   Three of them are brown.
   The rest are white.
   How many are white?

   12   8   6   NH
   ○   ○   ○   ○

   Draw or write to solve.

Use with text pages 25–27.

Addition Stories

Tell a story about 🐷 🐷 🐷 and 🐷 🐷.
You can use two different colored counters.
If you work with a partner you can each tell a
different part of the story.
Write the numbers.

1.

___3___   ___2___   _____ in all

or: _____   _____   _____ in all

Test Prep

Fill in the ○ for the correct answer. NH means Not Here.

2. The counters and numbers should match.

Which set of counters match the numbers?

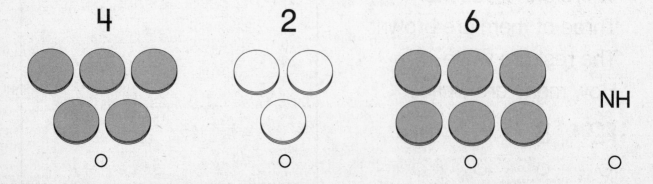

4   2   6   NH

○   ○   ○   ○

Use with text pages 35–36.

Name _____ Date _____

Model Addition

Use Workmat 3 and two different colored counters.
Show the parts. Find the whole.

1.

2.

Test Prep

Fill in the ○ for the correct answer. NH means Not Here.

3. Find the whole.

3   5   4   NH
○   ○   ○   ○

Explain how you used the counters to add.

_____

_____

Use with text pages 37–38.

Name _____ Date _____

Use Symbols to Add

Write the sum.

1.

   2 + 3 = __5__

2.

   1 + 3 = ____

3.

   2 + 4 = ____

4.

   3 + 1 = ____

Test Prep

5. Fill in the ○ for the correct answer. NH means Not Here.
   Which sum matches the picture?

   5 + 1 = ?

   4   3   6   NH
   ○   ○   ○   ○

Explain how you found the sum of 5 and 1.

_____

_____

Use with text pages 39–40.

Add With Zero

Write the sum.

1. $2 + 0 =$ __2__

2. $2 + 4 =$ ___

3. $1 + 5 =$ ___

4. $2 + 3 =$ ___

5. $0 + 1 =$ ___

6. $5 + 0 =$ ___

7. $0 + 3 =$ ___

8. $4 + 0 =$ ___

9. $1 + 4 =$ ___

10. $3 + 3 =$ ___

11. $2 + 4 =$ ___

12. $6 + 0 =$ ___

Test Prep

Fill in the ○ for the correct answer. NH means Not Here.

13. $0 + 5 =$?

0   3   5   NH
○   ○   ○   ○

Explain what happened when you added 0 and 5.

_____

Use with text pages 41–42.

Add in Any Order

Use cubes in two colors. Make the train.
Complete the two addition sentences for the train.

1. Make a 5 train.

$$\underline{}\ +\ \underline{}\ =\ \underline{}$$

$$\underline{}\ +\ \underline{}\ =\ \underline{}$$

2. Make a 6 train.

$$\underline{}\ +\ \underline{}\ =\ \underline{}$$

$$\underline{}\ +\ \underline{}\ =\ \underline{}$$

Add. Then change the order and complete
a new addition sentence.

3. $5 + 1 =$ _____

$$\underline{}\ +\ \underline{}\ =\ \underline{}$$

4. $4 + 1 =$ _____

$$\underline{}\ +\ \underline{}\ =\ \underline{}$$

5. $2 + 0 =$ _____

$$\underline{}\ +\ \underline{}\ =\ \underline{}$$

6. $2 + 3 =$ _____

$$\underline{}\ +\ \underline{}\ =\ \underline{}$$

Test Prep

Fill in the ○ for the correct answer. NH means Not Here.

7. $2 + 1 = 3 \qquad 1 + 2 = ?$

3   0   2   NH

○   ○   ○   ○

Use with text pages 45–46.

Ways to Make 7 and 8

Use two colors to show a way to make 7.
Complete the addition sentence.

1.

___ + ___ = _7_

Use two colors to show a way to make 8.
Complete the addition sentence.

2.

___ + ___ = ___

Test Prep

Fill in the ○ for the correct answer. NH means Not Here.

3. 5 + 2 = ?

5	7	4	NH
○	○	○	○

Explain your answer.

Use with text pages 47–48.

Add in Vertical Form

Complete the addition fact.

1. $+ \begin{matrix} 5 \\ 6 \end{matrix}$

2. $+$ ☐ / ☐

3. $+$ ☐ / ☐

Write the sum.

4. $\begin{matrix} 3 \\ +2 \end{matrix}$

5. $\begin{matrix} 2 \\ +4 \end{matrix}$

6. $\begin{matrix} 4 \\ +3 \end{matrix}$

7. $\begin{matrix} 3 \\ +5 \end{matrix}$

8. $\begin{matrix} 5 \\ +0 \end{matrix}$

Test Prep

Fill in the ○ for the correct answer. NH means Not Here.

9. $\begin{matrix} 1 \\ +7 \end{matrix}$

7   6   8   NH
○   ○   ○   ○

Explain how adding across and adding down are the same.

_____

Use with text pages 49–50.

Problem Solving
Write a Number Sentence

Write the addition sentence.
Write the answer.

1.

$4 \oplus 2 \ominus 6$

There are **4** rabbits eating.
Then **2** more rabbits come.
How many rabbits in all?   __6__ rabbits

2.

___ ◯ ___ ◯ ___

There are **3** butterflies.
Then **4** butterflies join them.
How many butterflies in all?   _____ butterflies

Test Prep

Fill in the ○ for the correct answer. NH means Not Here.

3.

$4 + 4 = ?$

There are **4** bugs on a leaf.
Then **4** bugs join them.
How many bugs in all?

8   4   6   NH
○   ○   ○   ○

Use with text pages 51–53.

Name _____ Date _____

Subtraction Stories

1. Ethan saw **4** birds in the bird bath.
   One of the birds flew away.
   Use counters to show the story and write the numbers.

_____   _____ flew away _____ are left

Test Prep

Fill in the ○ for the correct answer. NH means Not Here.

2. 1 + 3 = ☐

  4   3   2   NH
  ○   ○   ○   ○

Use with text pages 61–62.

Name _____ Date _____

Model Subtraction

Use Workmat 3 and counters.
Show the red part. Find the yellow part.
Write how many yellow.

1.

2.

3.

4.

Test Prep

Fill in the ○ for the correct answer. NH means Not Here.

5. There are 5 birds in all. Then 3 birds fly away.
   How many birds are left?

   2   3   4   NH
   ○   ○   ○   ○

Use with text pages 63–64.

Name _____ Date _____

Use Symbols to Subtract

Circle and cross out to subtract.

Write how many are left.

1.

   5 − 1 = ___

2.

   6 − 2 = ___

3. ⬭ ⬭ ⬭ ⬭

   4 − 3 = ___

4. ╱ ╱ ╱ ╱ ╱ ╱

   6 − 3 = ___

✓ Test Prep

Fill in the ○ for the correct answer. NH means Not Here.

5. Allen has 4 . He gives 2 away.
   How many does he have left?

   4   3   2   NH
   ○   ○   ○   ○

Explain how you got the answer.

_____

_____

Use with text pages 65–66.

Write Subtraction Sentences

Write the subtraction sentence.

1. _6_ ◯ _3_ ◯ _3_

2. ___ ◯ ___ ◯ ___

3. ___ ◯ ___ ◯ ___

4. ___ ◯ ___ ◯ ___

Write the difference.

5. $5 - 4 = $ _____

6. $5 - 3 = $ _____

7. $3 - 2 = $ _____

8. $6 - 2 = $ _____

9. $2 - 1 = $ _____

10. $4 - 3 = $ _____

Test Prep

Fill in the ◯ for the correct answer. NH means Not Here.

11. There are 6 🧒 on the team. Then 1 🧒 goes home.
How many 🧒 are still playing?

2   7   4   NH
◯   ◯   ◯   ◯

Explain how you arrived at your answer.

Use with text pages 67–68.

Zero in Subtraction

Write the difference.

1.

$2 - 2 =$ _____

2.

$4 - 4 =$ _____

3.

$6 - 0 =$ _____

4.

$3 - 3 =$ _____

5. $1 - 1 =$ _____

6. $3 - 0 =$ _____

7. $5 - 5 =$ _____

8. $2 - 0 =$ _____

9. $6 - 6 =$ _____

10. $1 - 0 =$ _____

Test Prep

Fill in the ○ for the correct answer. NH means Not Here.

11. Martin has 5 ✏️. He doesn't lose any of them.
How many does he have left?

0   1   5   NH
○   ○   ○   ○

Explain what happens when you subtract zero
from a number.

_____

_____

Use with text pages 71–72.

Subtract from 8 or Less

Use 8 cubes. Snap off some.

Circle and cross out the ones you snapped off.

Write the subtraction sentence.

1.

_____ – _____ = _____

2.

_____ – _____ = _____

3.

_____ – _____ = _____

Test Prep

Fill in the ○ for the correct answer. NH means Not Here.

4. Ed makes a tower with 8 blocks.
   Then 3 fall off.
   How many blocks are left?

   8   4   3   NH
   ○   ○   ○   ○

Use with text pages 73–74.

Name _____ Date _____

Subtract in Vertical Form

Complete the subtraction fact.

1.

```
  6
- 4
―――
  2
```

2.

```
  ☐
- ☐
―――
  ☐
```

Write the difference.

3.	4.	5.	6.	7.	8.
7	3	4	3	5	2
− 7	− 0	− 2	− 2	− 5	− 2

Test Prep

Fill in the ○ for the correct answer. NH means Not Here.

9. Jody has 7 . She mails 6 .

How many does she have left?

7   1   5   NH
○   ○   ○   ○

Complete the subtraction fact
you used to solve the problem.

```
  ☐
- ☐
―――
  ☐
```

Use with text pages 75–76.

22

Name _____ Date _____

Problem Solving
Act It Out With Models

Act out the problem with counters.
Write the answer.

1. Joanne has 7 party balloons. Then 3 balloons pop. How many balloons are left?

   __4__ balloons

Draw or write to explain.

2. Beth has 8 party hats and 2 hats are blue. How many hats are not blue?

   _____ hats

Test Prep

Fill in the ○ for the correct answer. NH means Not Here.

3. James gets 6 presents. He opens 3 of them. How many presents are unopened?

   9   5   3   NH
   ○   ○   ○   ○

Use with text pages 77–80.

Activity: Make a Tally Chart

1. Use the picture. Complete the tally chart. Cross out a picture and write **I** tally mark for each animal you cross out.

	Animals
	IIII IIII

Use the tally chart to solve.

2. How many are there?

_____

3. How many are there?

_____

---

4. Which has the most? Circle.

5. Which has the fewest? Circle.

 Test Prep

Fill in the ○ for the correct answer. NH means Not Here.

6. How many and ![] are there in all?

I I	8	5	NH
○	○	○	○

Use with text pages 87–88.

Read a Pictograph

Kinds of Fruit	Children Who Like Each Fruit
🍎	😊😊😊😊😊😊😊
🍌	😊😊😊😊
🍊	😊😊😊😊

Use the pictograph to solve.
Each 😊 stands for 1 child.

1. How many children
   like ?

   __4__ children

2. Which fruit do most
   children like? Circle.

     🍎

3. Which two fruits do the
   same number of children
   like? Circle.

   🍌 🍎 🍊

4. How many children like
   🍌 and 🍊 ?

   _____ children

Test Prep

Fill in the ○ for the correct answer. NH means Not Here.

5. How many children like apples?

   7   8   11   NH
   ○   ○   ○   ○

Use with text pages 89–90.

Make a Pictograph

1. Use the picture. Make a pictograph.

	Toys
🧸	☺ ☺ ☺ ☺
🐘	
🐢	

Use the pictograph to solve.

2. How many more than are there?

_____ more

3. How many and are there?

_____

Test Prep

Fill in the ○ for the correct answer. NH means Not Here.

4. How many 🧸 and 🐘 are there in all?

10   6   8   NH
○   ○   ○   ○

Use with text pages 91–92.

Name _____ Date _____

Read a Bar Graph

The bar graph shows how many children have each kind of pet.

Pets We Have

Number of Children

7
6
5
4
3
2
1
0

Kinds of Pets

Use the bar graph to solve.

1. Circle the pet 3 children have.

2. Do fewer children have or ? Circle.

3. How many children have a or a ?

_____

4. How many more children have than ?

_____ more

Test Prep

Fill in the ○ for the correct answer. NH means Not Here.

5. If 1 more child had a cat, how many children would have cats?

4   5   6   NH
○   ○   ○   ○

Use with text pages 95–96.

Name _____ Date _____

Activity: Make a Bar Graph

1. Use the picture. Make a bar graph.

Use the bar graph to solve.

2. How many more than ![kayak] are there?

_____ more

Fill in the ○ for the correct answer. NH means Not Here.

3. How many ![kayak] and ![bike] are there altogether?

3	7	2	NH
○	○	○	○

Use with text pages 97–99.

Name _____ Date _____

Problem Solving
Use a Graph

Use the bar graph to solve.

Books We Have Read

	0	1	2	3	4	5	6	7
Dinosaur Dig								
The Silly School								
My Mysteries								

Number of Children

1. How many more children read *Dinosaur Dig* than *The Silly School*?

   __2__ more children

   Draw or write to explain.

2. How many children in all read either *Dinosaur Dig* or *The Silly School*?

   _____ in all

Test Prep

Fill in the ○ for the correct answer. NH means Not Here.

3. How many more children would have to read *Dinosaur Dig* to have the same number as *My Mysteries*?

   1   3   4   NH
   ○   ○   ○   ○

Use with text pages 101–104.

Name _____ Date _____

Count On to Add

Count on to add.

1. $5 + 3 =$ __8__

2. $6 + 1 =$ ____

3. $7 + 3 =$ ____

4. $5 + 2 =$ ____

5. $8 + 1 =$ ____

6. $\begin{array}{r} 7 \\ +1 \\ \hline \end{array}$
7. $\begin{array}{r} 6 \\ +3 \\ \hline \end{array}$
8. $\begin{array}{r} 5 \\ +1 \\ \hline \end{array}$
9. $\begin{array}{r} 4 \\ +2 \\ \hline \end{array}$
10. $\begin{array}{r} 8 \\ +2 \\ \hline \end{array}$
11. $\begin{array}{r} 4 \\ +1 \\ \hline \end{array}$

12. $\begin{array}{r} 3 \\ +1 \\ \hline \end{array}$
13. $\begin{array}{r} 2 \\ +3 \\ \hline \end{array}$
14. $\begin{array}{r} 6 \\ +4 \\ \hline \end{array}$
15. $\begin{array}{r} 3 \\ +2 \\ \hline \end{array}$
16. $\begin{array}{r} 6 \\ +2 \\ \hline \end{array}$
17. $\begin{array}{r} 7 \\ +2 \\ \hline \end{array}$

✓ Test Prep

Fill in the ○ for the correct answer. NH means Not Here.

18. 4 puppies are inside.

How many puppies are there?

6   5   4   NH
○   ○   ○   ○

Explain how you got your answer.

_____

_____

Use with text pages 125–126.

Use a Number Line to Add

Find the sum.

1. $4 + 2 =$ ___6___   2. $6 + 1 =$ ___   3. $8 + 2 =$ ___

4. $5 + 3 =$ ___   5. $2 + 1 =$ ___   6. $7 + 2 =$ ___

7. $\begin{array}{r} 5 \\ +2 \\ \hline \end{array}$ 8. $\begin{array}{r} 6 \\ +3 \\ \hline \end{array}$ 9. $\begin{array}{r} 1 \\ +7 \\ \hline \end{array}$ 10. $\begin{array}{r} 3 \\ +5 \\ \hline \end{array}$ 11. $\begin{array}{r} 8 \\ +1 \\ \hline \end{array}$ 12. $\begin{array}{r} 7 \\ +3 \\ \hline \end{array}$

13. $\begin{array}{r} 2 \\ +7 \\ \hline \end{array}$ 14. $\begin{array}{r} 5 \\ +1 \\ \hline \end{array}$ 15. $\begin{array}{r} 3 \\ +6 \\ \hline \end{array}$ 16. $\begin{array}{r} 4 \\ +3 \\ \hline \end{array}$ 17. $\begin{array}{r} 6 \\ +2 \\ \hline \end{array}$ 18. $\begin{array}{r} 3 \\ +7 \\ \hline \end{array}$

Test Prep

Fill in the ○ for the correct answer. NH means Not Here.

19. Carrie wants to add $2 + 6$.
    What is the sum?

    30   7   8   NH
    ○   ○   ○   ○

Explain your answer.   What number should Carrie count
on from? Why?

_____

_____

Use with text pages 127–128.

Name _____ Date _____

Use Doubles to Add

Write the sum.

1. $2 + 2 = \underline{4}$ 2. $2 + 3 = \underline{}$ 3. $3 + 2 = \underline{}$

4. $3 + 3 = \underline{}$ 5. $3 + 4 = \underline{}$ 6. $4 + 3 = \underline{}$

---

7. $\begin{array}{r} 5 \\ +3 \\ \hline \end{array}$
8. $\begin{array}{r} 6 \\ +2 \\ \hline \end{array}$
9. $\begin{array}{r} 1 \\ +8 \\ \hline \end{array}$
10. $\begin{array}{r} 3 \\ +0 \\ \hline \end{array}$
11. $\begin{array}{r} 8 \\ +2 \\ \hline \end{array}$
12. $\begin{array}{r} 7 \\ +1 \\ \hline \end{array}$

---

13. $\begin{array}{r} 2 \\ +5 \\ \hline \end{array}$
14. $\begin{array}{r} 5 \\ +5 \\ \hline \end{array}$
15. $\begin{array}{r} 6 \\ +3 \\ \hline \end{array}$
16. $\begin{array}{r} 4 \\ +4 \\ \hline \end{array}$
17. $\begin{array}{r} 6 \\ +0 \\ \hline \end{array}$
18. $\begin{array}{r} 3 \\ +6 \\ \hline \end{array}$

Test Prep

Fill in the ○ for the correct answer.

NH means Not Here.

19. Jason has 3 pens.

Alice has 3 pens.

How many pens do they have?

3   6   8   NH
○   ○   ○   ○

Use with text pages 129–130.

32

Using Addition Strategies

Write the sum.

1.
$$\begin{array}{r} 1 \\ +3 \\ \hline 4 \end{array}$$

2.
$$\begin{array}{r} 4 \\ +5 \\ \hline \end{array}$$

3.
$$\begin{array}{r} 2 \\ +8 \\ \hline \end{array}$$

4.
$$\begin{array}{r} 9 \\ +0 \\ \hline \end{array}$$

5.
$$\begin{array}{r} 7 \\ +2 \\ \hline \end{array}$$

6.
$$\begin{array}{r} 3 \\ +2 \\ \hline \end{array}$$

7.
$$\begin{array}{r} 3 \\ +5 \\ \hline \end{array}$$

8.
$$\begin{array}{r} 6 \\ +4 \\ \hline \end{array}$$

9.
$$\begin{array}{r} 6 \\ +3 \\ \hline \end{array}$$

10.
$$\begin{array}{r} 1 \\ +3 \\ \hline \end{array}$$

11.
$$\begin{array}{r} 8 \\ +0 \\ \hline \end{array}$$

12.
$$\begin{array}{r} 5 \\ +5 \\ \hline \end{array}$$

13. $5 + 3 =$ _____

14. $7 + 1 =$ _____

15. $2 + 7 =$ _____

16. $6 + 2 =$ _____

17. $4 + 5 =$ _____

18. $6 + 0 =$ _____

Test Prep

Fill in the ○ for the correct answer. NH means Not Here.

19. Mom has 5 stamps. She buys 2 more.
    How many stamps does she have now?

    3   7   8   NH
    ○   ○   ○   ○

Explain how you found the answer.

_____

_____

Use with text pages 133–134.

Practice
5.5

Problem Solving: Write a Number Sentence

Use Workmat 3 and counters.
Write a number sentence to solve.

1. The Tigers score 2 runs.
   The Bears score 3 runs.
   How many runs are
   there altogether?

   ___ ◯ ___ ◯ ___

2. Alice has 4 stickers.
   Jenna has 4 stickers.
   How many stickers are
   there in all?

   ___ ◯ ___ ◯ ___

Test Prep

Fill in the ○ for the correct answer. NH means Not Here.

3. There are 5 girls and 5 boys on the team.
   How many children are on the team?

   9   0   10   NH
   ○   ○   ○   ○

Explain how you found the answer.

_____

_____

Use with text pages 135–138.

Name _____ Date _____

Count Back to Subtract

Count back to subtract.

1. 7 − 3 = __4__   2. 9 − 2 = ____

3. 8 − 3 = ____   4. 10 − 1 = ____   5. 6 − 2 = ____

6. 9 − 3 = ____   7. 8 − 2 = ____   8. 10 − 3 = ____

9. 10   10. 5   11. 7   12. 8   13. 5
  − 2   − 2   − 2   − 1   − 3

14. 5   15. 7   16. 4   17. 3   18. 10
  − 1   − 1   − 3   − 1   − 3

Test Prep

Fill in the ○ for the correct answer. NH means Not Here.

19. Subtract.   10
                 − 3

8   7   6   NH
○   ○   ○   ○

Explain how counting back helped you find the answer.

_____

Use with text pages 145–146.

Use a Number Line to Subtract

Write the difference.

1. $7 - 2 = \underline{5}$

2. $6 - 3 = \underline{}$

3. $9 - 1 = \underline{}$

4. $5 - 2 = \underline{}$

5. $4 - 1 = \underline{}$

6. $6 - 2 = \underline{}$

7. $\begin{array}{r} 10 \\ -\ 2 \\ \hline \end{array}$

8. $\begin{array}{r} 5 \\ -2 \\ \hline \end{array}$

9. $\begin{array}{r} 7 \\ -2 \\ \hline \end{array}$

10. $\begin{array}{r} 8 \\ -1 \\ \hline \end{array}$

11. $\begin{array}{r} 5 \\ -3 \\ \hline \end{array}$

12. $\begin{array}{r} 4 \\ -3 \\ \hline \end{array}$

13. $\begin{array}{r} 10 \\ -\ 1 \\ \hline \end{array}$

14. $\begin{array}{r} 5 \\ -3 \\ \hline \end{array}$

15. $\begin{array}{r} 6 \\ -1 \\ \hline \end{array}$

16. $\begin{array}{r} 10 \\ -\ 3 \\ \hline \end{array}$

Test Prep

Fill in the ○ for the correct answer. NH means Not Here.

17. Subtract.
$\begin{array}{r} 9 \\ -2 \\ \hline \end{array}$

5   6   7   NH

○   ○   ○   ○

Use with text pages 147–148.

Name _____ Date _____

How Many More? How Many Fewer?

Match. Then subtract.

1. How many more than 👟?

   9 – 6 = __3__

2. How many fewer 🧣 than 🎩?

   8 – 3 = _____

3. How many more ⊙ than ▦?

   10 – 6 = _____

4. How many more ☕ than ◯?

   7 – 2 = _____

Test Prep

Fill in the ○ for the correct answer. NH means Not Here.

5. Subtract.   7
              – 5

   3   2   1   NH
   ○   ○   ○   ○

Explain how matching helped you find how many more or how many fewer.

_____

_____

Use with text pages 149–150.

Practice
6.4

Relate Addition and Subtraction

Use ⬚, ⬚, and Workmat 3.

Show the parts. Complete the related facts.

1.

Whole
?

Part	Part

$6 + 3 = \underline{9}$

$9 - 3 = \underline{6}$

2.

Whole
?

Part	Part

$2 + 5 = \underline{}$

$7 - 2 = \underline{}$

---

3. $6 + 3 = \underline{}$ **4.** $5 + 3 = \underline{}$ **5.** $2 + 7 = \underline{}$

$9 - 3 = \underline{}$ $8 - 3 = \underline{}$ $9 - 7 = \underline{}$

---

6. $1 + 3 = \underline{}$ **7.** $8 + 2 = \underline{}$ **8.** $4 + 4 = \underline{}$

$4 - 3 = \underline{}$ $10 - 2 = \underline{}$ $8 - 4 = \underline{}$

Test Prep

Fill in the ○ for the correct answer.

NH means Not Here.

9. Which set of numbers shows the related facts?

Whole	
Part	**Part**

$6 + 2 = 8$ $7 + 3 = 10$ $4 + 5 = 9$

$9 - 3 = 6$ $9 - 2 = 7$ $9 - 5 = 4$ NH

○   ○   ○   ○

Use with text pages 153–154.

Fact Families

Use ⬚, ⬚, and Workmat 3. Complete the fact family.

1.

Whole
7

Part	Part
4	3

$\underline{4} + \underline{3} = \underline{7}$ $\underline{7} - \underline{3} = \underline{4}$

$\underline{3} + \underline{4} = \underline{7}$ $\underline{7} - \underline{4} = \underline{3}$

2.

Whole
8

Part	Part
5	3

___ + ___ = ___   ___ − ___ = ___

___ + ___ = ___   ___ − ___ = ___

3.

Whole
10

Part	Part
6	4

___ + ___ = ___   ___ − ___ = ___

___ + ___ = ___   ___ − ___ = ___

4.

Whole
6

Part	Part
4	2

___ + ___ = ___   ___ − ___ = ___

___ + ___ = ___   ___ − ___ = ___

Test Prep

Fill in the ○ for the correct answer.

5. Which set of numbers shows the related facts?

$5 + 2 = 7$	$3 + 3 = 6$	$1 + 7 = 8$
$2 + 5 = 7$	$2 + 3 = 5$	$7 + 2 = 9$
$7 - 2 = 5$	$5 - 2 = 3$	$8 - 7 = 1$
$7 - 5 = 2$	$6 - 3 = 3$	$9 - 2 = 7$
○	○	○

Whole
7

Part	Part
5	2

Use with text pages 155–156.

Name _____ Date _____

Using Subtraction Strategies

Write the difference.

> **Ways to Subtract**
> Count back. Use counters.
> Use a related addition fact.

1. $4 - 0 = \underline{4}$ 2. $7 - 2 = \underline{}$ 3. $9 - 6 = \underline{}$

4. $5 - 4 = \underline{}$ 5. $8 - 6 = \underline{}$ 6. $6 - 4 = \underline{}$

7. $\begin{array}{r} 5 \\ -5 \\ \hline \end{array}$ 8. $\begin{array}{r} 8 \\ -5 \\ \hline \end{array}$ 9. $\begin{array}{r} 10 \\ -10 \\ \hline \end{array}$ 10. $\begin{array}{r} 4 \\ -3 \\ \hline \end{array}$ 11. $\begin{array}{r} 7 \\ -3 \\ \hline \end{array}$ 12. $\begin{array}{r} 6 \\ -5 \\ \hline \end{array}$

13. $\begin{array}{r} 7 \\ -4 \\ \hline \end{array}$ 14. $\begin{array}{r} 6 \\ -3 \\ \hline \end{array}$ 15. $\begin{array}{r} 10 \\ -9 \\ \hline \end{array}$ 16. $\begin{array}{r} 8 \\ -3 \\ \hline \end{array}$ 17. $\begin{array}{r} 6 \\ -1 \\ \hline \end{array}$ 18. $\begin{array}{r} 9 \\ -9 \\ \hline \end{array}$

19. $\begin{array}{r} 9 \\ -5 \\ \hline \end{array}$ 20. $\begin{array}{r} 10 \\ -0 \\ \hline \end{array}$ 21. $\begin{array}{r} 3 \\ -1 \\ \hline \end{array}$ 22. $\begin{array}{r} 9 \\ -7 \\ \hline \end{array}$ 23. $\begin{array}{r} 4 \\ -2 \\ \hline \end{array}$ 24. $\begin{array}{r} 8 \\ -7 \\ \hline \end{array}$

Test Prep

Fill in the ○ for the correct answer. NH means Not Here.

25. Subtract. $\begin{array}{r} 10 \\ -6 \\ \hline \end{array}$ 5   4   3   NH
                                  ○   ○   ○   ○

Explain how you found $10 - 6$.

_____

Use with text pages 157–158.

Problem Solving: Choose the Operation

Choose the operation to solve.

1. There were 7 puppies sleeping. 4 puppies woke up. How many puppies were still sleeping?

Draw or write to explain.

___3___ puppies

2. 3 kittens play with a ball. 4 more come to play. How many kittens are playing now?

_____ kittens

3. The dog herded 3 cows from one field. Then it herded 5 cows from another field. How many cows did the dog herd in?

_____ cows

 Test Prep

Fill in the ○ for the correct answer. NH means Not Here.

4. There are 8 puppy treats. 3 of the treats are eaten. How many puppy treats are left?

3   4   5   NH
○   ○   ○   ○

Use with text pages 159–160.

Name _____ Date _____

Classifying and Sorting Objects

Tell how the shells are alike.
Write color, size, or shape.

1. _____ color _____

2. _____

Test Prep

Fill in the ○ for the correct answer. NH means Not Here.

3.

Which bead belongs in the group above?

 ○   ◻ ○   ▲ ○   NH ○

Use with text pages 183–184.

Name _____ Date _____

Plane Shapes

1. Color the triangles [🖍 Red].

2. Color the circles [🖍 Black].

3. Color the square [🖍 Blue].

4. Color the rectangles [🖍 Yellow].

Test Prep

Fill in the ○ for the correct answer. NH means Not Here.

5. Which shape has **3** sides and **3** corners?

⬜   ⬠   △   NH

○   ○   ○   ○

Use with text pages 185–186.

Name _____ Date _____

Classifying and Sorting Shapes

Read the sorting rule.
Circle the shapes that follow each rule.

1. Shapes with corners

2. Shapes with 3 corners

3. Shapes with more than 3 sides

Test Prep

Fill in the ○ for the correct answer. NH means Not Here.

4. Adam made a group of these shapes.

What was his sorting rule?

Large shapes	Small shapes	Square shapes	NH
○	○	○	○

Use with text pages 187–188.

Activity: Solid Shapes

Circle the solid that matches.

1. 0 edges

_____

2. 5 faces

Complete the table. Use solid shapes.
Write the number of faces, edges, and corners.

	Number of Faces	Number of Edges	Number of Corners
3. cube	6	12	8
4. sphere			
5. cylinder			
6. cone			

✓ Test Prep

Fill in the ○ for the correct answer. NH means Not Here.

7. I am a shape that can roll and stack. What shape am I?

sphere   cylinder   cube   NH

○   ○   ○   ○

Use with text pages 191–192.

Name _____ Date _____

Classifying and Sorting Solid Shapes

rectangle   rectangular prism   sphere   pyramid   circle

square   cylinder   cone   triangle   cube

Sort the shapes. Write the name.

1. **Plane Shapes**	2. **Solid Shapes**
circle	
_____	_____
_____	_____
_____	_____
	_____
	_____

Test Prep

Fill in the ○ for the correct answer. NH means Not Here.

3. I am a solid shape with **6** faces. What am I?

            NH

○   ○   ○   ○

Use with text pages 193–194.

Name _____   Date _____

Identify Faces of a Solid Shape

Look at the plane shape.
Circle the solid with a face like it.

Test Prep

Fill in the ○ for the correct answer. NH means Not Here.

5. Which solid does NOT have a face that is a square?

      NH

○   ○   ○   ○

Use with text pages 195–196.

Name _____ Date _____

Problem Solving
Draw a Picture

1. Essie wants to make 4 △ ☐ from this piece of cloth. How can she cut the cloth?

Draw your picture here.

2. Show the clown head that Jeb made from these pieces.

Test Prep

3. Fill in the ○ for the correct answer. NH means Not Here.

Which pieces made these steps?

         NH

○   ○   ○   ○

Use with text pages 197–199.

Position Words

Follow the directions.

Draw the object.

1. Draw an 🌰 to the right of 🐿️ .

2. Draw a ☀️ over the 🌳 .

3. Draw a 🌸 between the 🏠 and the 🏠 .

4. Draw 3 🍎 under the 🌳 .

Test Prep

Fill in the ○ for the correct answer. NH means Not Here.

5. In the picture above, where is the 🐿️ ?

left of the 🌳
○

between the 🌳 and the 🏠
○

over the 🌳
○

NH
○

Use with text pages 207–208.

More Position Words

Circle the answer that completes the sentence.

1.

The 🐕 is _____ the 🏠.

(in front of)   behind

2.

The 🐱 is _____ the 🌳.

up   down

3.

The ⛵ is _____ the 🛶.

far from   near

4.

The 🐱 is _____ the 🐕.

far from   next to

Test Prep

Fill in the ○ for the correct answer. NH means Not Here.

5. Use the word behind, near, or up to complete the sentence.

The 🪣 is _____ the 🏰.

up   behind   near   NH
○   ○   ○   ○

Use with text pages 209–210.

Name _____ Date _____

Give and Follow Directions

Follow the directions.

Draw an object on the grid.

Go Right →	Go Up ↑	Draw
1. 2 spaces	4 spaces	
2. 5 spaces	2 spaces	☼
3. 4 spaces	4 spaces	🌳

Test Prep

Fill in the ○ for the correct answer. NH means Not Here.

4. Look at the grid. Go right 2 spaces. Go up 4 spaces.
   What is next to the ?

                        NH

   ○   ○   ○   ○

Use with text pages 211–212.

Name _____ Date _____

Slides, Flips, and Turns

Use pattern blocks.

Put your block on the shape.

Move and trace your block to show a flip, a turn, and a slide.

1. Flip

2. Turn

3. Slide

Test Prep

Fill in the ○ for the correct answer. NH means Not Here.

4. Look at this figure.

   Which figure below shows a flip?

   ┐   ⌐   L   NH
   ○   ○   ○   ○

Use with text pages 215–218.

Patterns

Use shapes to copy the pattern.
Circle the one that comes next.

1. △ ☐ △ ☐ △ ☐ | △ ☐

2. ○ ☐ ○ ☐ ○ ☐ | ○ ☐

3. ○ ∘ ○ ∘ ○ ∘ | ○ ∘

4. ● ○ ● ○ ● ○ | ● ○

Test Prep

Fill in the ○ for the correct answer. NH means Not Here.

5. Which comes next?

▲ △ ◭ ▲ △ ◭ ▲ △ ◭

               NH
  ○   ○   ○   ○

Use with text pages 219–220.

Create Patterns

Use the shapes to draw a pattern.

1.

2.

3.

 Test Prep

Fill in the ○ for the correct answer. NH means Not Here.

4. Which might come next?

D   D   D   NH

○   ○   ○   ○

Use with text pages 221–222.

Name _____ Date _____

Symmetry

Draw a line of symmetry.

1.

2.

3.

4.

5.

6. 8

7.

8.

9.

Test Prep

Fill in the ○ for the correct answer. NH means Not Here.

10. Which shows a line of symmetry?

         NH

○   ○   ○   ○

Use with text pages 223–225.

Name _____ Date _____

Problem Solving
Find a Pattern

Solve.

1. Becky makes this pattern on a belt.
   Put an **X** on the shape that is wrong in the pattern.
   Draw the correct shape.

2. Bella makes a necklace with this pattern.
   Circle the shape that comes next.

 Test Prep

Fill in the ○ for the correct answer. NH means Not Here.

3. Look at the pattern.
   Which figure comes next?

          □   ▨   NH

   ○   ○   ○   ○

Use with text pages 227–230.

Equal Parts

1. Circle the shape that shows equal parts.

Write the number of equal parts.

2.

_____ equal parts

3.

_____ equal parts

4.

_____ equal parts

5.

_____ equal parts

6.

_____ equal parts

7.

_____ equal parts

Test Prep

Fill in the ○ for the correct answer. NH means Not Here.

8. Which shape has **3** equal parts?

           NH

○   ○   ○   ○

Use with text pages 237–238.

Name _____ Date _____

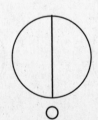

One Half

Color $\frac{1}{2}$:

1.

2.

3.

4.

5.

6.

Draw a line to show halves.

7.

8.

9.

Test Prep

Fill in the ○ for the correct answer. NH means Not Here.

10. Debbie wants $\frac{1}{2}$ a pizza.

Which picture shows halves?

○   ○   ○   NH
              ○

Practice 9.2

Use with text pages 239–240.

One Fourth

Color $\frac{1}{4}$.

1.

2.

3.

4.

5.

6.

Draw lines to show fourths.

7.

8.

9.

Test Prep

Fill in the ○ for the correct answer. NH means Not Here.

10. Jill wants one fourth of an apple. How many equal pieces will the apple be divided into?

   4   3   2   NH
   ○   ○   ○   ○

Explain how dividing in half can help you find a fourth.

_____

_____

_____

Use with text pages 241–242.

Name _____ Date _____

Fractions of a Set

Color to show the fraction.

1. $\frac{1}{3}$

2. $\frac{1}{2}$

3. $\frac{1}{4}$

4. $\frac{1}{3}$

5. $\frac{1}{2}$

6. $\frac{1}{4}$

Test Prep

Fill in the ○ for the correct answer. NH means Not Here.

7. Which set shows $\frac{1}{4}$?

   NH

○   ○   ○   ○

Use with text pages 245–246.

Name _____ Date _____

Activity: Probability

1. Use a .
   Drop the penny 10 times.
   See which side of the penny
   shows each time.
   Record your tries here.

Side	Tally
Heads	
Tails	

2. Look at this spinner. What
   letter do you predict you would
   spin most often? _____
   Check your prediction. Spin 10 times.
   Record your spins.

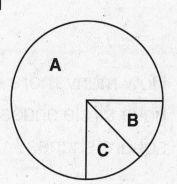

Letter	Tally
A	
B	
C	

Test Prep

Fill in the ○ for the correct answer. NH means Not Here.

3. Pam spins this spinner. What
   number is she most likely to spin?

  1   2   3   NH

  ○   ○   ○   ○

Use with text pages 247–250.

Problem Solving Use a Picture

Use the picture to solve.

1. Emma takes a cookie without looking. Which shape is she more likely to pick?

Draw or write to explain.

_____

2. How many more cookies have circle shapes than square shapes?

_____ more cookies have circle shapes.

3. Kelly takes a cracker from the bag. Is she more likely to take a large cracker or a small cracker?

_____

Use with text pages 251–254.

Name _____ Date _____

Count Tens

Write the number of tens.
Write the number.

1. _____ 4 tens
_____ 40
forty

2. _____ tens
_____
fifty

3. _____ tens
_____
sixty

Test Prep

Fill in the ○ for the correct answer.

4. This is one set of cubes.
How many in 7 sets?

7   10   17   70
○   ○   ○   ○

Use with text pages 277–278.

63

Tens and Ones

Use Workmat 5 and ⬚.

Show.	Regroup. Write the tens and the ones.	Write the number.
1. 32 ones	___3___ tens ___2___ ones	___32___
2. 15 ones	_____ ten _____ ones	_____
3. 40 ones	_____ tens _____ ones	_____
4. 12 ones	_____ ten _____ ones	_____
5. 29 ones	_____ tens _____ ones	_____
6. 41 ones	_____ tens _____ one	_____
7. 18 ones	_____ ten _____ ones	_____
8. 37 ones	_____ tens _____ ones	_____
9. 22 ones	_____ tens _____ ones	_____

Test Prep

Fill in the ○ for the correct answer. NH means Not Here.

10. What word names the missing number?

sixteen _____ eighteen

seventeen   fifteen   eleven   NH

○   ○   ○   ○

Use with text pages 279–280.

Numbers Through 50

Use Workmat 5, , and ⬜ .
Show and write the tens and the ones.
Write the number.

1.

Workmat 5	
Tens	Ones

_2_ tens
_7_ ones
_27_
twenty-seven

2.

Workmat 5	
Tens	Ones

____ tens
____ ones
____
thirty-five

3.

Workmat 5	
Tens	Ones

____ tens
____ ones
____
forty-nine

4.

Workmat 5	
Tens	Ones

____ tens
____ ones
____
forty-one

Test Prep

Fill in the ○ for the correct answer. NH means Not Here.

5. How many in all?

13   23   33   NH
○   ○   ○   ○

Explain your answer.

Use with text pages 281–282.

Name _____ Date _____

Place Value Through 99

Write the tens in the tens place.
Write the ones in the ones place.
Write the number.

1.

Tens	Ones
3	5

35

2.

Tens	Ones

_____

3.

Tens	Ones

_____

4.

Tens	Ones

_____

Test Prep

Fill in the ○ for the correct answer.

5. How many tens are there in the number 95?

90   19   10   9
○   ○   ○   ○

Use with text pages 287–288.

Different Ways to Show Numbers

Write the number in different ways.

1.

___3___ tens ___4___ ones

___30___ + ___4___ = ___34___

2.

_____ tens _____ ones

_____ + _____ = _____

3.

_____ tens _____ one

_____ + _____ = _____

4.

_____ tens _____ ones

_____ + _____ = _____

5.

_____ tens _____ ones

_____ + _____ = _____

Test Prep

Fill in the ○ for the correct answer.

6. What is another way to write 5 tens and 6 ones?

65   56   55   50

○   ○   ○   ○

Use with text pages 289–290.

Name _____ Date _____

Numbers Through 100

Write how many tens and ones. Write the number.

1.

___1___ ten ___3___ ones

___13___ thirteen

2.

_____ tens _____ ones

_____ eighty-four

3.

_____ tens _____ ones

_____ sixty

4.

_____ tens _____ ones

_____ seventy-six

Test Prep

Fill in the ○ for the correct answer. NH means Not Here.

5. What is another way to write 10 tens?

1   10   100   NH
○   ○   ○   ○

Use with text pages 291–292.

Name _____ Date _____

Problem Solving
Act It Out With Models

Use ⬭⬭⬭⬭ and ◻ to solve.

Draw or write to explain.

1. Rick puts 43 action figures in cases. Each case holds 10 action figures. How many cases does Rick use?

_5_ cases

2. Ling puts 36 muffins in boxes. Each box holds 10 muffins. How many boxes does Ling need?

_____ boxes

Test Prep

Fill in the ○ for the correct answer.

3. Gina puts 47 books in a bookcase. 10 books fit on each shelf. How many shelves does she use?

4   5   7   10
○   ○   ○   ○

Explain your answer.

Use with text pages 293–296.

Name _____ Date _____

Order Numbers

Use Workmats 7 and 8.

Write the number that comes just before or just after.

1. __72__ , 73   2. 77, _____   3. _____ , 81

4. 83, _____   5. _____ , 71   6. _____ , 80

Write the number that comes between.

7. 72, _____ , 74   8. 79, _____ , 81   9. 75, _____ , 77

10. 77, _____ , 79   11. 80, _____ , 82   12. 74, _____ , 76

Write the missing numbers.
Count forward or backward.

13. 42, _____ , _____ , 45   14. 19, _____ , _____ , 16

15. 62, _____ , _____ , 65   16. 37, _____ , _____ , 40

Test Prep

Fill in the ○ for the correct answer. NH means Not Here.

17. Marisa sits in the seat between 24 and 26.
    What is her seat number?

    2   25   27   NH
    ○   ○   ○   ○

Use with text pages 303–304.

Name _____ Date _____

Ordinal Numbers

Color.

1. first

Black

2. third

Red

3. seventh

Green

4. second

Brown

5. ninth

Yellow

6. fifth

Blue

7. first

Red

8. tenth

Blue

9. sixth

Brown

10. fourth

Yellow

11. eighth

Green

12. second

Black

Test Prep

Fill in the ○ for the correct answer.

13. Terry is fifth in line. Avi is in front of her.
In what place in line is Avi?

sixth   fifth   fourth   third
  ○   ○   ○   ○

Use with text pages 305–306.

Use Ten to Estimate

Circle one group of ten. Estimate about how many in all.
Then count.

1.

Estimate
20
Count
17

2.

Estimate
_____
Count
_____

3.

Estimate
_____
Count
_____

Test Prep

Fill in the ○ for the correct answer.
NH means Not Here.

4. Jan dropped her crayons. About
   how many crayons does she have?

about 10   about 20   about 30   NH
   ○   ○   ○   ○

Use with text pages 307–310.

Name _____ Date _____

Greater Than, Less Than

Circle the number that is greater.

1.   42   33

2.   26   29

3.   90   80

4.   54   55

Circle the number that is less.

5.   51   15

6.   39   40

7.   70   77

8.   98   68

Test Prep

Fill in the ○ for the correct answer. NH means Not Here.

9. Lindsey has 35 markers.

   Nick has fewer markers than Lindsey.

   How many markers does Nick have?

   53   40   30   NH
   ○   ○   ○   ○

Use with text pages 311–312.

Name _____ Date _____

Use Symbols to Compare Numbers

Compare. Circle >, <, or =.

1. >
 <
 =

2. >
 <
 =

3. >
 <
 =

4. >
 <
 =

5. >
 <
 =

6. >
 <
 =

7. >
 <
 =

8. >
 <
 =

 Test Prep

Fill in the ○ for the correct answer.

9. Maria's basket has 46 apples.
 The number in Mike's basket is
 equal to the number in Maria's basket.
 How many apples are in Mike's basket?

 40   46   50   64
 ○   ○   ○   ○

Use with text pages 313–314.

Name _____ Date _____

Problem Solving:
Reasonable Answers

Estimate. Circle the answer that makes sense.

1. Kate goes to see a movie.

   About how long is the movie?

   (about 2 hours)

   about 10 hours

2. First graders take a bus trip.

   About how many children sit in the bus?

   about 3 children

   about 30 children

3. Ellen baby-sits her younger brother.

   About how old is her brother?

   about 6 years old

   about 16 years old

4. Ben bakes some muffins.

   About how many cups of flour does he use?

   about 2 cups

   about 22 cups

5. Eli reads a book before going to bed. He starts after taking his bath. About how many hours does Eli read?

   about 11 hours

   about 1 hour

Use with text pages 315–316.

Name _____ Date _____

Count by Twos

Write the missing numbers.
Skip count by 2s.

1	2	3	4	5	6	7	8	9	10
11	12	13	14	15	16	17	18	19	20
21	22	23	24	25	26	27	28	29	30
31	32	33	34	35	36	37	38	39	40
41	42	43	44	45	46	47	48	49	50
51	52	53	54	55	56	57	58	59	60
61	62	63	64	65	66	67	68	69	70
71	72	73	74	75	76	77	78	79	80
81	82	83	84	85	86	87	88	89	90
91	92	93	94	95	96	97	98	99	100

1. 18, _20_, _22_, 24

2. 32, 34, _____, _____, 40

3. 64, _____, _____, 70

4. 46, 48, _____, _____

5. 54, _____, _____, 60

6. 86, _____, _____, _____, _____, _____

7. 54, _____, _____, 60, _____, _____

8. 92, _____, _____, _____, _____

9. Skip count by 2s from 22 to 50.

Use to color the numbers you say.

Test Prep

Fill in the ○ for the correct answer.

10. If you count by 2s from 20 to 50,
    which number would you say?

   23   44   52   66
   ○   ○   ○   ○

Use with text pages 323–324.

Count by Fives

Write the missing numbers.
Skip count by 5s.

1	2	3	4	5	6	7	8	9	10
11	12	13	14	15	16	17	18	19	20
21	22	23	24	25	26	27	28	29	30
31	32	33	34	35	36	37	38	39	40
41	42	43	44	45	46	47	48	49	50
51	52	53	54	55	56	57	58	59	60
61	62	63	64	65	66	67	68	69	70
71	72	73	74	75	76	77	78	79	80
81	82	83	84	85	86	87	88	89	90
91	92	93	94	95	96	97	98	99	100

1. 25, __30__, __35__, __40__

2. 30, 35, _____, _____, 50

3. 55, _____, _____, 70

4. 70, _____, _____, 85

5. 60, _____, _____, _____

6. 80, _____, _____, _____, _____

Count back by 5s.

7. 65, 60, _____, _____, _____, 40

8. 30, _____, _____, _____, _____, _____, 0

9. Skip count by 5s from 50 to 100.

Use ⟨▭⟩ to color the numbers you say.

Test Prep

Fill in the ○ for the correct answer. NH means Not Here.

10. If you count by 5s from 20 to 80,
     which number would you say?

    5   15   100   NH
    ○   ○   ○   ○

Use with text pages 325–326.

Name _____ Date _____

More Than, Less Than

Write the number that is 1 more.

1. 39 __40__   2. 77 _____

3. 53 _____   4. 80 _____

1	2	3	4	5	6	7	8	9	10
11	12	13	14	15	16	17	18	19	20
21	22	23	24	25	26	27	28	29	30
31	32	33	34	35	36	37	38	39	40
41	42	43	44	45	46	47	48	49	50
51	52	53	54	55	56	57	58	59	60
61	62	63	64	65	66	67	68	69	70
71	72	73	74	75	76	77	78	79	80
81	82	83	84	85	86	87	88	89	90
91	92	93	94	95	96	97	98	99	100

Write the number that is 1 less.

5. _____ 30   6. _____ 58

7. _____ 86   8. _____ 100

Write the number that is 10 more.

9. 21   10. 45   11. 57   12. 60   13. 83

_____   _____   _____   _____   _____

Write the number that is 10 less.

14. _____   15. _____   16. _____   17. _____   18. _____

25   30   53   71   89

Test Prep

Fill in the ○ for the correct answer.

19. Mary has 23 dolls.
    Susan has 10 more than Mary.
    How many dolls does Susan have?

    43   33   23   13
    ○   ○   ○   ○

Use with text pages 327–328.

Odd and Even Numbers

Circle odd or even.

1. 13

⬚⬚⬚⬚⬚⬚⬚
⬚⬚⬚⬚⬚⬚

(odd)   even

2. 18

⬚⬚⬚⬚⬚⬚⬚⬚⬚
⬚⬚⬚⬚⬚⬚⬚⬚⬚

odd   even

3. 9

⬚⬚⬚⬚⬚
⬚⬚⬚⬚

odd   even

4. 6

⬚⬚⬚
⬚⬚⬚

odd   even

5. 10

⬚⬚⬚⬚⬚
⬚⬚⬚⬚⬚

odd   even

6. 17

⬚⬚⬚⬚⬚⬚⬚⬚⬚
⬚⬚⬚⬚⬚⬚⬚⬚

odd   even

7. Color the even numbers 🖍 Yellow .

Color the odd numbers 🖍 Purple .

51	52	53	54	55	56	57	58	59	60
61	62	63	64	65	66	67	68	69	70
71	72	73	74	75	76	77	78	79	80

Test Prep

Fill in the ○ for the correct answer. NH means Not Here.

8. Which number is an odd number?

36   53   88   NH

○   ○   ○   ○

Use with text pages 331–332.

Problem Solving
Find a Pattern

Find the pattern. Solve.

1. Jack walks his dog 2 times each day. How many times does he walk the dog in 5 days?

Day 1	Day 2	Day 3	Day 4	Day 5
2				
He walks the dog _____ times.				

2. Susie reads 5 books each week. How many books does she read in 5 weeks?

Week 1	Week 2	Week 3	Week 4	Week 5
She reads _____ books.				

Test Prep

Fill in the ○ for the correct answer.

3. Tammy reads 10 pages of her book each day. How many pages will she read in 6 days?

   60   50   40   10
   ○   ○   ○   ○

Explain how you found your answer.

_____

_____

Use with text pages 333–336.

Name _____ Date _____

Order Events

Write 1, 2, and 3 to show the correct order.

1.   [2]   [3]   [1]

2.   [ ]   [1]   [ ]

3.   [ ]   [ ]   [ ]

 Test Prep

Fill in the ○ for the correct answer. NH means Not Here.

4. Jane is sending a postcard to a friend.
   What is the last thing she will do?

Write the   Put the postcard   Put a stamp on   NH
postcard.   in the mailbox.   the postcard.

   ○   ○   ○   ○

Use with text pages 359–360.

Name _____ Date _____

Activity: Estimate a Minute

Circle activities you know take about 1 minute.
Draw an X on the activity if it takes more than 1 minute.

1.

2.

3.

4.

Test Prep

Fill in the ○ under the correct answer. NH means Not Here.

5. Which of these activities takes more than 1 minute?

      NH

○   ○   ○   ○

Use with text pages 361–362.

ock. **Write the time two ways.**

1.

4 o'clock

2.

_____ o'clock

3.

_____ o'clock

4.

_____ o'clock

5.

_____ o'clock

6.

_____ o'clock

Test Prep

Fill in the ○ for the correct answer. NH means Not Here.

7. What time is it on the clock?

 12:00   8:00   2:00   NH

○   ○   ○   ○

Use with text pages 363–364.

Name _____ Date _____

Half-Hour

Say and write the time.

1.

__10__ o'clock

2.

half past _____

3.

half past _____

4.

_____ o'clock

Test Prep

Fill in the ○ for the correct answer. NH means Not Here.

5. Abby begins reading at 5:30.
Which clock shows the time?

   NH

○   ○   ○   ○

Use with text pages 365–368.

Elapsed Time

Use a clock.

Show when the activity starts or ends.

Start	How long?	End
1.	I hour reading	[:]
2. [:]	I hour cooking	**6:00**
3.	2 hours driving	[:]

Test Prep

Fill in the ○ for the correct answer. NH means Not Here.

4. The movie starts at **5:00**. It lasts **2** hours.
  What time is it over?

○   ○   ○   ○ NH

Use with text pages 369–372.

Name _____ Date _____

Practice Telling Time

Show the time on the clock.

1. I get up at 7 o'clock.

2. I eat breakfast at half past 7.

3. I help mom at half past 8.

4. I walk the dog at 11 o'clock.

Test Prep

Fill in the ○ for the correct answer. NH means Not Here.

5. Phillip gets home at 4 o'clock.
   Which clock shows the time?

NH

○ ○ ○ ○

Use with text pages 373–374.

Name _____ Date _____

Days and Weeks

Fill in the calendar for this month.

Saturday	Monday	Tuesday	Wednesday	Thursday	Friday	Saturday

1. Color today ⬛ Red ⬛ .

2. What is the date of the second Monday
   in this month? _____

3. What day is the last day in this month? _____

Test Prep

Fill in the ○ for the correct answer. NH means Not Here.

4. Andrew's birthday is on June 5.
   His party is two days later.
   What is the date of his party?

   June 3   June 6   June 7   NH

   ○   ○   ○   ○

Use with text pages 375–376.

Name _____ Date _____

Months

Use the calendars to find the answer.

August
S	M	T	W	T	F	S
		1	2	3	4	5
6	7	8	9	10	11	12
13	14	15	16	17	18	19
20	21	22	23	24	25	26
27	28	29	30	31		

September
S	M	T	W	T	F	S
					1	2
3	4	5	6	7	8	9
10	11	12	13	14	15	16
17	18	19	20	21	22	23
24	25	26	27	28	29	30

October
S	M	T	W	T	F	S
1	2	3	4	5	6	7
8	9	10	11	12	13	14
15	16	17	18	19	20	21
22	23	24	25	26	27	28
29	30	31				

1. Which month has 5 Fridays? _September_

2. School begins on September 6. Color it green.

3. Use (⫘ Red ⫘⟩. Color all Tuesdays in October.

4. Use (⫘ Blue ⫘⟩. Color August 10.

Test Prep

Fill in the ○ for the correct answer. NH means Not Here.

5. Lily goes on a trip on Friday.
   She comes back 2 days later.
   On which day does she come back?

   Sunday   Saturday   Thursday   NH
     ○   ○   ○   ○

Use with text pages 377–378.

Name _____ Date _____

Problem Solving Use a Table

Use the table to solve the problem.

Monday Schedule

Activity	Time
Reading	9:00
Math	11:00
Lunch	12:00
Science	1:00
Art	2:00
Dismissal	3:00

Draw or write to explain.

1. Ms. Roper gets to school at **8:00**. How much time does she have before Reading?

_____ hour _____

2. What activity starts **2** hours before Science?

_____

3. What activity starts **2** hours after lunch?

_____

4. How many hours are there between Reading and Lunch?

_____

Use with text pages 379–382.

Name _____ Date _____

Value of Coins

Find the value of the coins.

1.

___1___¢   ___2___¢   ___3___¢   ___4___¢   ___5___¢   [5] ¢

2.

_____¢   _____¢   _____¢   _____¢   _____¢   [   ] ¢

3.

_____¢   _____¢   _____¢   _____¢   _____¢   _____¢   [   ] ¢

Test Prep

Fill in the ○ for the correct answer. NH means Not Here.

4. What is the value of the coins?

50¢   40¢   80¢   NH
○   ○   ○   ○

Use with text pages 389–390.

Name _____ Date _____

Nickels and Pennies

Find the value of the coins.

1.

__5__ ¢ __10__ ¢ __11__ ¢ __12__ ¢ __13__ ¢ __14__ ¢ | 14 | ¢

2.

_____ ¢ _____ ¢ _____ ¢ _____ ¢ _____ ¢ _____ ¢ [   ] ¢

3.

_____ ¢ _____ ¢ _____ ¢ _____ ¢ _____ ¢ _____ ¢ [   ] ¢

Test Prep

Fill in the ○ for the correct answer. NH means Not Here.

4. What is the value of the coins?

23¢   33¢   28¢   NH
  ○   ○   ○   ○

Use with text pages 391–392.

Name _____ Date _____

Dimes and Pennies

Circle the group of coins that matches the price.

1. 32¢

---

2. 40¢

---

3. 23¢

---

4. 41¢

Test Prep

Fill in the ○ for the correct answer. NH means Not Here.

5. What is the value of the coins?

23¢   43¢   18¢   NH
○   ○   ○   ○

Use with text pages 393–394.

Name _____ Date _____

Count Coins

Use coins.

Find the value of the coins.

1. ___32___ ¢

2. _____ ¢

3. _____ ¢

4. _____ ¢

✓ Test Prep

Fill in the ○ for the correct answer. NH means Not Here.

5. What is the value of the coins?

33¢   58¢   41¢   NH
○   ○   ○   ○

Use with text pages 395–396.

Name _____ Date _____

Quarters

Use coins.

Circle the coins that match the price.

![Test Prep]

Fill in the ○ for the correct answer. NH means Not Here.

5. What price matches the coins?

46¢   41¢   36¢   NH

○   ○   ○   ○

Use with text pages 399–401.

Name _____ Date _____

Practice 14.6

Equal Amounts

Use coins.
Complete the chart.

	Show the amount with coins.	Show another way.
12¢	5¢ 5¢ 1¢ 1¢	10¢ 1¢ 1¢
32¢	10¢ 10¢ 10¢ 1¢ 1¢	25¢ 5¢ 1¢ 1¢
27¢	25¢ 1¢ 1¢	10¢ 10¢ 5¢ 1¢ 1¢
45¢	25¢ 10¢ 10¢	10¢ 10¢ 10¢ 10¢ 5¢

Test Prep

Fill in the ○ for the correct answer. NH means Not Here.

What is one way to show 25¢?

                  NH

○   ○   ○   ○

Use with text pages 403–404.

Problem Solving Use a Picture

Use coins to solve.

1. Rafael wants to buy the lion.
   He has 15¢.
   What other coins might he use
   to buy the lion?

2. Eric wants to buy the pencil case.
   He has 2 dimes and a nickel.
   How many more dimes does
   he need?

Test Prep

Fill in the ○ for the correct answer. NH means Not Here.

3. Leo has a quarter and 3 nickels. How much more does
   he need to buy juice for 50¢?

   5¢   10¢   25¢   NH
   ○   ○   ○   ○

Use with text pages 405–408.

Count On to Add

Use the number line.
Write the sum.

1. $5 + 3 =$ ___ 8   2. $9 + 2 =$ ___   3. $8 + 4 =$ ___

4. $4 + 1 =$ ___   5. $7 + 5 =$ ___   6. $3 + 8 =$ ___

7. $6 + 2 =$ ___   8. $9 + 1 =$ ___   9. $7 + 1 =$ ___

10. $8 + 2 =$ ___   11. $5 + 4 =$ ___   12. $9 + 3 =$ ___

13. $2 + 7 =$ ___   14. $3 + 4 =$ ___   15. $4 + 6 =$ ___

Test Prep

Fill in the ○ for the correct answer. NH means Not Here.

16. Shawn had 6 pennies. He found 4 more pennies. How many pennies did he have in all?

8	10	12	NH
○	○	○	○

Explain your answer.

Use with text pages 429–430.

Name _____ Date _____

Sums of 10

Use Workmat 1 and ◯ to make 10.
Draw counters to fill the ten frame.
Complete the addition sentence.

1.

2.

$6 +$ __4__ $= 10$

$5 +$ ___ $= 10$

Write the sum.

3. $3 + 7 =$ ___

4. $0 + 9 =$ ___

5. $6 + 2 =$ ___

6. $3 + 3 =$ ___

7. $8 + 1 =$ ___

8. $4 + 5 =$ ___

Test Prep

Fill in the ○ for the correct answer. NH means Not Here.

9. There are 10 spaces on a game board. Ben has moved 7 spaces. How many spaces does he still have to move?

Explain your answer.

7   5   3   NH
○   ○   ○   ○

Use with text pages 431–432.

Sums of 11

Use Workmat 1 and ⬡ to make 11.
Complete the addition sentence.

1. 6 + __5__ = 11

2. 8 + ___ = 11

Write the sum.

3. 7 + 4 = ___
4. 5 + 6 = ___
5. 3 + 8 = ___

6. 9 + 2 = ___
7. 4 + 7 = ___
8. 2 + 9 = ___

9.
```
  6     5
+ 5   + 6
```

10.
```
  8     2
+ 2   + 8
```

11.
```
  7     4
+ 4   + 7
```

Test Prep

Fill in the ○ for the correct answer. NH means Not Here.

12. Adam has 5 books about
    sports. He has 6 books
    about animals. How many
    books does he have in all?

    8   9   10   NH
    ○   ○   ○   ○

Explain your answer.

Use with text pages 433–434.

Sums of 12

Write the sum.

1.
$$7 \quad 5$$
$$+5 \quad +7$$
$$12 \quad 12$$

2.
$$6 \quad 2$$
$$+2 \quad +6$$

3.
$$4 \quad 6$$
$$+6 \quad +4$$

4.
$$8 \quad 3$$
$$+3 \quad +8$$

5.
$$3 \quad 4$$
$$+4 \quad +3$$

6.
$$7 \quad 3$$
$$+3 \quad +7$$

7.
$$3 \quad 5$$
$$+5 \quad +3$$

8.
$$8 \quad 4$$
$$+4 \quad +8$$

9.
$$6 \quad 5$$
$$+5 \quad +6$$

10. $4 + 3 =$ _____

3 + 4 = _____

11. $1 + 8 =$ _____

8 + 1 = _____

12. $9 + 0 =$ _____

0 + 9 = _____

Test Prep

Fill in the ○ for the correct answer. NH means Not Here.

13. Brendan needs 12 nails for a project. He has 9 nails. How many more nails does he need?

5   4   3   NH
○   ○   ○   ○

Use with text pages 435–436.

Addition Facts Practice

Use any strategy.
Find the sum.

1. $6 + 6 =$ __12__   2. $3 + 7 =$ ___   3. $2 + 5 =$ ___

4. $1 + 9 =$ ___   5. $4 + 6 =$ ___   6. $5 + 3 =$ ___

7. $\begin{array}{r} 1 \\ +5 \\ \hline \end{array}$
8. $\begin{array}{r} 3 \\ +2 \\ \hline \end{array}$
9. $\begin{array}{r} 7 \\ +2 \\ \hline \end{array}$
10. $\begin{array}{r} 8 \\ +4 \\ \hline \end{array}$
11. $\begin{array}{r} 9 \\ +3 \\ \hline \end{array}$
12. $\begin{array}{r} 8 \\ +2 \\ \hline \end{array}$

13. $\begin{array}{r} 2 \\ +4 \\ \hline \end{array}$
14. $\begin{array}{r} 5 \\ +6 \\ \hline \end{array}$
15. $\begin{array}{r} 7 \\ +3 \\ \hline \end{array}$
16. $\begin{array}{r} 4 \\ +5 \\ \hline \end{array}$
17. $\begin{array}{r} 5 \\ +5 \\ \hline \end{array}$
18. $\begin{array}{r} 6 \\ +3 \\ \hline \end{array}$

Test Prep

Fill in the ○ for the correct answer. NH means Not Here.

19. Pat has 5 pencils. Doug has twice as many pencils. How many pencils does Doug have?

1   10   8   NH
○   ○   ○   ○

Use with text pages 439–442.

Name _____ Date _____

Add Three Numbers

Write the sum.

1.
$$
\begin{array}{r}
1 \\
3 \\
+4 \\
\hline
8
\end{array}
$$

2.
$$
\begin{array}{r}
3 \\
5 \\
+4 \\
\hline
\end{array}
$$

3.
$$
\begin{array}{r}
7 \\
0 \\
+4 \\
\hline
\end{array}
$$

4.
$$
\begin{array}{r}
6 \\
1 \\
+4 \\
\hline
\end{array}
$$

5.
$$
\begin{array}{r}
5 \\
2 \\
+3 \\
\hline
\end{array}
$$

6.
$$
\begin{array}{r}
4 \\
1 \\
+5 \\
\hline
\end{array}
$$

7.
$$
\begin{array}{r}
2 \\
4 \\
+4 \\
\hline
\end{array}
$$

8.
$$
\begin{array}{r}
3 \\
5 \\
+1 \\
\hline
\end{array}
$$

9.
$$
\begin{array}{r}
7 \\
1 \\
+3 \\
\hline
\end{array}
$$

10.
$$
\begin{array}{r}
2 \\
9 \\
+0 \\
\hline
\end{array}
$$

11.
$$
\begin{array}{r}
3 \\
3 \\
+5 \\
\hline
\end{array}
$$

12.
$$
\begin{array}{r}
6 \\
2 \\
+1 \\
\hline
\end{array}
$$

13. $7 + 2 + 2 =$ _____

14. $2 + 7 + 1 =$ _____

15. $2 + 3 + 1 =$ _____

16. $4 + 2 + 1 =$ _____

Test Prep

Fill in the ○ for the correct answer. NH means Not Here.

17. Hans has 5 stamps. He buys 2 more stamps. His mother gives him 4 more stamps. How many stamps does he have now?

9   11   7   NH
○   ○   ○   ○

Explain your answer.

Use with text pages 443–444.

Missing Addends

Use cubes.

Find the missing addend.

1. □○□○□○□○□○□○□○

$$\boxed{3} + 4 = 7$$

2. □○□○□○□○□○□○□○□○

$$\boxed{} + 6 = 8$$

3. $5 + \boxed{} = 8$ 4. $2 + \boxed{} = 10$ 5. $3 + \boxed{} = 11$

6. $\begin{array}{r} 1 \\ + \boxed{} \\ \hline 8 \end{array}$
7. $\begin{array}{r} 4 \\ + \boxed{} \\ \hline 6 \end{array}$
8. $\begin{array}{r} \boxed{} \\ + 3 \\ \hline 10 \end{array}$
9. $\begin{array}{r} 6 \\ + \boxed{} \\ \hline 9 \end{array}$
10. $\begin{array}{r} \boxed{} \\ + 2 \\ \hline 11 \end{array}$

11. $\begin{array}{r} \boxed{} \\ + 4 \\ \hline 7 \end{array}$
12. $\begin{array}{r} \boxed{} \\ + 6 \\ \hline 12 \end{array}$
13. $\begin{array}{r} \boxed{} \\ + 3 \\ \hline 5 \end{array}$
14. $\begin{array}{r} \boxed{} \\ + 5 \\ \hline 10 \end{array}$
15. $\begin{array}{r} 2 \\ + \boxed{} \\ \hline 7 \end{array}$

Test Prep

Fill in the ○ for the correct answer. NH means Not Here.

16. Ethan has 10 model cars. 4 cars are red. How many cars are **not** red?

4   6   14   NH
○   ○   ○   ○

Explain your answer.

Use with text pages 445–446.

Problem Solving Make a Table

Complete the table. Solve.

Item   Numbers

Pens	
Pencils	3
Notebooks	
Markers	

Draw or write to explain.

1. How many pencils and pens are there?

   _____ pencils and pens

2. How many more markers than notebooks are there?

   _____ markers

3. If 3 markers are added, how many markers are there?

   _____ markers

Use with text pages 447–449.

Name _____ Date _____

Count Back to Subtract

```
    0   1   2   3   4   5   6   7   8   9   10   11   12
```

Use the number line.
Subtract.

1. 9   2. 7   3. 10   4. 6   5. 11   6. 8
   − 1   − 2   − 3   − 2   − 3   − 1
   ‾‾‾   ‾‾‾   ‾‾‾   ‾‾‾   ‾‾‾   ‾‾‾
    8

7. 5   8. 11   9. 9   10. 10   11. 9   12. 10
   − 2   − 2   − 3   − 2   − 2   − 1
   ‾‾‾   ‾‾‾   ‾‾‾   ‾‾‾   ‾‾‾   ‾‾‾

13. 8 − 3 = _____   14. 7 − 1 = _____   15. 11 − 1 = _____

Test Prep

Fill in the ○ for the correct answer. NH means Not Here.

16. Subtract.
            12
          − 2
          ‾‾‾‾

Explain your answer.

9   10   11   NH
○   ○   ○   ○

Use with text pages 457–458.

Subtract From 11 or Less

Write the difference.

Whole	
11	
Part	**Part**
9	?

Whole	
11	
Part	**Part**
5	?

Whole	
10	
Part	**Part**
2	?

1. $11 - 9 =$ _2_

   $11 - 2 =$ _9_

2. $11 - 5 =$ ___

   $11 - 6 =$ ___

3. $10 - 2 =$ ___

   $10 - 8 =$ ___

4.
```
  11     11
-  2   -  9
```

5.
```
  10     10
-  7   -  3
```

6.
```
  11     11
-  7   -  4
```

7.
```
   9      9
-  3   -  6
```

8.
```
  10     10
-  6   -  4
```

9.
```
  11     11
-  3   -  8
```

Test Prep

Fill in the ○ for the correct answer. NH means Not Here.

10. Subtract.

$10 - 7$

1   2   3   NH
○   ○   ○   ○

Explain your answer.

Use with text pages 459–460.

Subtract From 12 or Less

Write the difference.

Whole	
9	
Part	Part
3	?

Whole	
10	
Part	Part
9	?

Whole	
12	
Part	Part
5	?

1. $9 - 3 =$ _6_

   $9 - 6 =$ _3_

2. $10 - 9 =$ ___

   $10 - 1 =$ ___

3. $12 - 5 =$ ___

   $12 - 7 =$ ___

4. 12 12
   -4 -8

5. 11 11
   -8 -3

6. 9 9
   -7 -2

7. 12 12
   -3 -9

8. 10 10
   -8 -2

9. 11 11
   -5 -6

Test Prep

Fill in the ○ for the correct answer. NH means Not Here.

10. Subtract.

$12 - 5$

6   5   4   NH
○   ○   ○   ○

Explain your answer.

Use with text pages 461–462.

Relate Addition and Subtraction

Use related facts to add and subtract.

1. $\begin{array}{r} 7 \\ +4 \\ \hline \end{array}$ $\begin{array}{r} 11 \\ -7 \\ \hline \end{array}$
2. $\begin{array}{r} 6 \\ +3 \\ \hline \end{array}$ $\begin{array}{r} 9 \\ -6 \\ \hline \end{array}$
3. $\begin{array}{r} 9 \\ +3 \\ \hline \end{array}$ $\begin{array}{r} 12 \\ -9 \\ \hline \end{array}$

4. $\begin{array}{r} 6 \\ +6 \\ \hline \end{array}$ $\begin{array}{r} 12 \\ -6 \\ \hline \end{array}$
5. $\begin{array}{r} 7 \\ +5 \\ \hline \end{array}$ $\begin{array}{r} 12 \\ -7 \\ \hline \end{array}$
6. $\begin{array}{r} 6 \\ +4 \\ \hline \end{array}$ $\begin{array}{r} 10 \\ -4 \\ \hline \end{array}$

7. $\begin{array}{r} 5 \\ +4 \\ \hline \end{array}$ $\begin{array}{r} 9 \\ -4 \\ \hline \end{array}$
8. $\begin{array}{r} 2 \\ +9 \\ \hline \end{array}$ $\begin{array}{r} 11 \\ -2 \\ \hline \end{array}$
9. $\begin{array}{r} 7 \\ +2 \\ \hline \end{array}$ $\begin{array}{r} 9 \\ -2 \\ \hline \end{array}$

10. $\begin{array}{r} 7 \\ +3 \\ \hline \end{array}$ $\begin{array}{r} 10 \\ -7 \\ \hline \end{array}$
11. $\begin{array}{r} 2 \\ +8 \\ \hline \end{array}$ $\begin{array}{r} 10 \\ -8 \\ \hline \end{array}$
12. $\begin{array}{r} 8 \\ +4 \\ \hline \end{array}$ $\begin{array}{r} 12 \\ -4 \\ \hline \end{array}$

✔ Test Prep

Fill in the ○ for the correct answer. NH means Not Here.

13. Find the related subtraction sentence.

$$7 + 5 = 12$$

$12 - 6 = 6$ $12 - 5 = 7$ $12 - 4 = 8$ NH

○   ○   ○   ○

Use with text pages 465–466.

Fact Families for 11

Complete the fact family.

1.

11	
6	5

$6 + 5 =$ __11__ $11 - 6 =$ __5__

$5 + 6 =$ __11__ $11 - 5 =$ __6__

2.

9	
3	6

$3 + 6 =$ ____ $9 - 3 =$ ____

$6 + 3 =$ ____ $9 - 6 =$ ____

3.

11	
8	3

$8 + 3 =$ ____ $11 - 8 =$ ____

$3 + 8 =$ ____ $11 - 3 =$ ____

4.

11	
2	9

$2 + 9 =$ ____ $11 - 2 =$ ____

$9 + 2 =$ ____ $11 - 9 =$ ____

Test Prep

Fill in the ○ for the correct answer. NH means Not Here.

5. Complete the fact family.

11	
7	4

$7 + 4 = 11$ $11 - 7 = 4$

? $11 - 4 = 7$

$3 + 8 = 11$ $2 + 9 = 11$ $4 + 7 = 11$ NH

○   ○   ○   ○

Use with text pages 467–468.

Fact Families for 12

Complete the fact family.

1.
12	
9	3

$9 + 3 =$ __12__ $12 - 9 =$ ____

$12 - 3 =$ ____   ____ ◯ ____ = ____

2.
12	
5	7

$5 + 7 =$ ____ $12 - 5 =$ ____

$7 + 5 =$ ____   ____ ◯ ____ = ____

3.
11	
6	5

$11 - 6 =$ ____ $11 - 5 =$ ____

$5 + 6 =$ ____   ____ ◯ ____ = ____

Test Prep

Fill in the ◯ for the correct answer. NH means Not Here.

4. Complete the fact family.

12	
8	4

$8 + 4 = 12$ $4 + 8 = 12$

$12 - 4 = 8$?

$8 - 4 = 4$ $4 + 4 = 8$ $12 - 6 = 6$ NH
   ◯   ◯   ◯   ◯

Use with text pages 469–470.

Names for Numbers

Circle the names for the number.

1. $\boxed{7}$ $\left(5 + 2\right)$ $3 + 4$ $4 + 2 + 1$

   $12 - 7$ $7 - 2$ $6 + 0 + 2$

---

2. $\boxed{12}$ $12 - 0$ $3 + 8$ $5 + 3 + 4$

   $2 + 9$ $7 + 5$ $9 + 1 + 1$

---

3. $\boxed{6}$ $2 + 4$ $12 - 6$ $6 + 0 + 1$

   $3 + 3$ $7 - 2$ $3 + 1 + 2$

---

4. $\boxed{10}$ $12 - 3$ $9 + 1$ $5 + 5 + 1$

   $3 + 8$ $11 - 1$ $4 + 1 + 5$

Test Prep

Fill in the ○ for the correct answer. NH means Not Here.

5. Which choice does <u>not</u> name the number 11?

   $8 + 3$ $7 + 4$ $12 - 2$ NH

   ○   ○   ○   ○

Use with text pages 471–472.

Name _____ Date _____

Problem Solving
Choose the Operation

Add or subtract to solve.

1. There are 8 puppies asleep in the basket. Some of the puppies wake up. Now 5 puppies are still sleeping. How many puppies are awake? _____ puppies are awake.	Draw or write to explain.
2. There are 4 gray kittens in the yard. There are 4 orange kittens on the porch. How many kittens are there in both places? _____ kittens in both places	

Test Prep

Fill in the ○ for the correct answer. NH means Not Here.

3. Ramón sees 9 kittens in the pet shop window. He sees 6 puppies there, too. How many fewer puppies than kittens does Ramón see in the pet shop window?

3   4   5   NH
○   ○   ○   ○

Use with text pages 473–476.

Compare and Order Length

Is the object longer or shorter than your hand?

1.

(longer) shorter

2.

longer shorter

3.

longer shorter

4.

longer shorter

Number the objects in order from shortest to longest.

5.

____   ____   ____   ____

Test Prep

Fill in the ○ for the correct answer. NH means Not Here.

6. Which of these items is probably longer than your shoe?

pen   backpack   bar of soap   NH

○   ○   ○   ○

Use with text pages 499–500.

Name _____ Date _____

Nonstandard Units

Choose a unit to measure the length.
Write the measure. Circle the unit.

Find the object.	Measure	Unit

1.   about _____

2.   about _____

3.   about _____

4.   about _____

Test Prep

Fill in the ○ for the correct answer. NH means Not Here.

5. Use small paper clips.

Measure the length of the drawing.

1   3   4   NH
○   ○   ○   ○

Use with text pages 501–502.

Name _____ Date _____

Inches

Use the picture.
Complete the chart.

	1.	2.	3.	4.
Estimate	about ___ inches	about ___ inches	about ___ inches	about ___ inches
Measure	about 4 ___ inches	about ___ inch	about ___ inches	about ___ inch

Test Prep

Fill in the ○ for the correct answer. NH means Not Here.

5. Jade measured the length of her shoe.
   What is a reasonable measurement?

2 inches   7 inches   20 inches   NH
   ○   ○   ○   ○

Use with text pages 503–504.

Centimeters

Estimate. Then use a centimeter ruler to measure.

1.

Estimate: about _____ centimeters

Measure: about ___10___ centimeters

2.

Estimate: about _____ centimeters

Measure: about _____ centimeters

3.

Estimate: about _____ centimeters

Measure: about _____ centimeters

4.

Estimate: about _____ centimeters

Measure: about _____ centimeters

Test Prep

Fill in the ○ for the correct answer. NH means Not Here.

5. About how long is a pencil?

3 centimeters   15 centimeters   35 centimeters   NH

○   ○   ○   ○

Use with text pages 505–506.

Compare Weight

Choose a unit to measure the weight.
Write the measure. Circle the unit.

Find the object.	**Measure**	**Unit**

1.   about ____

---

2.   about ____

Number the objects in order from lightest to heaviest.

3.

____   ____   ____

Test Prep

Fill in the ○ for the correct answer. NH means Not Here.

4. Kim has a book, a key, and a pencil in her backpack.
Which is the heaviest?

book   key   pencil   NH
 ○   ○   ○   ○

Use with text pages 509–510.

Name _____ Date _____

Activity: Pounds

Circle.

Use if the object weighs
more than 1 pound.

Use if the object weighs
less than 1 pound.

1.

Test Prep

Fill in the ○ for the correct answer. NH means Not Here.

2. Clare goes shopping.
   Which item weighs about 1 pound?

   NH

   ○   ○   ○   ○

Use with text pages 511–512.

Kilograms

Circle.

Use if the object is more than 1 kilogram.

Use if the object is less than 1 kilogram.

1.

Test Prep

Fill in the ○ for the correct answer. NH means Not Here.

2. Which person is about 7 kilograms?

NH

    ○   ○   ○   ○

Use with text pages 513–514.

Problem Solving
Use Logical Reasoning

Solve.

Circle the pencil that matches the clues.

Cross out items to find the answer.

1. It has hearts.

   It is not the longest pencil.

2. It is shorter than the
   dog pencil.
   It has birds.

3. It has stripes.
   It has an eraser.

Use with text pages 515–516.

Name _____ Date _____

Compare and
Order Capacity

Number the objects.
I holds the least amount. 3 holds the greatest amount.

1.

_3_   _2_   _1_

2.

____   ____   ____

3.

____   ____   ____

Test Prep

Fill in the ○ for the correct answer. NH means Not Here.

4. Which holds the most?

                     NH

    ○   ○   ○   ○

Use with text pages 523–524.

Name _____ Date _____

Activity: Cups, Pints, and Quarts

Use cups, pints, and quarts to compare.
Circle which holds more.

1.

2.

3.

4.

Circle which can hold the same amount.

5.

6.

Test Prep

Fill in the ○ for the correct answer. NH means Not Here.

7. Which holds the same amount as these?

NH

Use with text pages 525–526.

Name _____ Date _____

Liters

Circle.

Use if the object can hold more than 1 liter.

Use if the object can hold less than 1 liter.

1.

Circle the containers that can hold more than 1 liter.

2.

Test Prep

Fill in the ○ for the correct answer. NH means Not Here.

3. Which holds less than 1 liter?

○   ○   ○   ○

Use with text pages 527–529.

Name _____ Date _____

Temperature

Circle **hot** or **cold** to tell about the temperature.

1. 85 degrees

(hot)   cold

2. 30 degrees

hot   cold

3. 25 degrees

hot   cold

4. 95 degrees

hot   cold

Test Prep

Fill in the ○ for the correct answer. NH means Not Here.

5. Which temperature is the coldest?

32 degrees   28 degrees   35 degrees   NH

○   ○   ○   ○

Use with text pages 531–532.

Problem Solving: Reasonable Answers

Circle the answer that makes more sense.

1. Alberto wants to know how long his kite string is. What can he use to measure?

2. Ramona needs to know which is lighter, a feather or a pencil. What can she use to find out?

Test Prep

Fill in the ○ for the correct answer. NH means not here.

3. Bess has a bag of marbles and a baseball. She wants to know which is heavier. What can she use to find out?

               NH

    ○   ○   ○   ○

Use with text pages 533–534.

Name _____ Date _____

Doubles Plus One

Find the sum.

Think
Use a double fact.
Add 1 more.

1. 5 + 5 = __10__   5 + 6 = __11__

2. 5
 +5

3. 1
 +1

4. 1
 +2

5. 5
 +6

6. 4
 +4

7. 5
 +4

8. 7
 +7

9. 7
 +8

10. 3
 +3

11. 4
 +3

12. 3
 +4

13. 10
 +9

14. 9
 +9

15. 8
 +9

16. 9
 +8

17. 4
 +5

18. 6
 +5

19. 8
 +7

Test Prep

20. There are 9 robins in a tree. There are 8 robins on a fence. How many robins are there in all?

_____ robins

Draw or write to explain.

Use with text pages 557–558.

Name _____ Date _____

Add With Ten

1. Show 10. Show 2 more.

10 ⊕ 2 ⊟ 12

2. Show 10. Show 6 more.

___ ◯ ___ ◯ ___

3. Show 10. Show 1 more.

___ ◯ ___ ◯ ___

4. Show 10. Show 9 more.

___ ◯ ___ ◯ ___

Find the sum.

5. 10
      + 4

6. 10
      + 8

7.   5
      + 10

8.   1
      + 10

9.   4
      + 10

10.   6
      + 10

11. 10
      + 3

12. 10
      + 6

13. 10
      + 5

14. 10
      + 2

Test Prep

Fill in the ○ for the correct answer.

15.

Workmat 2

Which number sentence tells about the counters?

○ $10 + 10 = 20$

○ $10 + 6 = 16$

○ $10 + 5 = 15$

○ $10 + 1 = 11$

Use with text pages 559–560.

Name _____ Date _____

Make a Ten to Add

Use Workmat 2 and ◯.
Make a ten.
Find the sum.

1. Show 8 and 7 more.

   $8 + 7 = \underline{15}$

2. Show 6 and 8 more.

   $6 + 8 = \underline{}$

3. Show 9 and 3 more.

   $9 + 3 = \underline{}$

4. Show 7 and 9 more.

   $7 + 9 = \underline{}$

Add.

5. $\begin{array}{r} 8 \\ +8 \\ \hline \end{array}$
6. $\begin{array}{r} 6 \\ +8 \\ \hline \end{array}$
7. $\begin{array}{r} 9 \\ +3 \\ \hline \end{array}$
8. $\begin{array}{r} 7 \\ +9 \\ \hline \end{array}$
9. $\begin{array}{r} 9 \\ +7 \\ \hline \end{array}$
10. $\begin{array}{r} 4 \\ +9 \\ \hline \end{array}$

11. $\begin{array}{r} 7 \\ +6 \\ \hline \end{array}$
12. $\begin{array}{r} 7 \\ +8 \\ \hline \end{array}$
13. $\begin{array}{r} 3 \\ +8 \\ \hline \end{array}$
14. $\begin{array}{r} 5 \\ +9 \\ \hline \end{array}$
15. $\begin{array}{r} 9 \\ +2 \\ \hline \end{array}$
16. $\begin{array}{r} 7 \\ +7 \\ \hline \end{array}$

Test Prep

17. Paul has 8 pennies. Dena has 5 pennies. Make a ten and show how many pennies they have in all.

    _____ pennies

Draw or write to explain.

Use with text pages 561–562.

Name _____ Date _____

Addition Practice

Choose a way to add.
Find the sum.

> Use parts and
> wholes. Make a ten.
> Use a double fact.

1. $6 + 4 = \underline{10}$ 2. $9 + 7 = \underline{\hphantom{00}}$ 3. $5 + 5 = \underline{\hphantom{00}}$

4. $\begin{array}{r} 6 \\ + 6 \\ \hline \end{array}$ 5. $\begin{array}{r} 1 \\ + 8 \\ \hline \end{array}$ 6. $\begin{array}{r} 10 \\ + 2 \\ \hline \end{array}$ 7. $\begin{array}{r} 4 \\ + 9 \\ \hline \end{array}$ 8. $\begin{array}{r} 8 \\ + 6 \\ \hline \end{array}$ 9. $\begin{array}{r} 3 \\ + 2 \\ \hline \end{array}$

10. $\begin{array}{r} 9 \\ + 9 \\ \hline \end{array}$ 11. $\begin{array}{r} 4 \\ + 7 \\ \hline \end{array}$ 12. $\begin{array}{r} 2 \\ + 8 \\ \hline \end{array}$ 13. $\begin{array}{r} 10 \\ + 9 \\ \hline \end{array}$ 14. $\begin{array}{r} 5 \\ + 8 \\ \hline \end{array}$ 15. $\begin{array}{r} 5 \\ + 9 \\ \hline \end{array}$

16. $\begin{array}{r} 7 \\ + 6 \\ \hline \end{array}$ 17. $\begin{array}{r} 5 \\ + 6 \\ \hline \end{array}$ 18. $\begin{array}{r} 7 \\ + 5 \\ \hline \end{array}$ 19. $\begin{array}{r} 8 \\ + 8 \\ \hline \end{array}$ 20. $\begin{array}{r} 7 \\ + 7 \\ \hline \end{array}$ 21. $\begin{array}{r} 8 \\ + 7 \\ \hline \end{array}$

Test Prep

Fill in the ○ for the correct answer.
NH means Not Here.

22. Ben has 9 pieces of a puzzle.
    Dee has the other 6 puzzle pieces.
    How many pieces are in the whole puzzle?

    3 pieces   15 pieces   16 pieces   NH

Use with text pages 565–566.

Name _____ Date _____

Names for Numbers

Use Workmat 3 and ◯ .

Find different names for the number.

1.

Whole
12

Part	Part
5	7

Whole
12

Part	Part

Whole
12

Part	Part

Whole
12

Part	Part

2.

Whole
15

Part	Part

Whole
15

Part	Part

3.

Whole
14

Part	Part

Whole
14

Part	Part

4.

Whole
13

Part	Part

Whole
13

Part	Part

5.

Whole
16

Part	Part

Whole
16

Part	Part

✓ Test Prep

Fill in the ○ for the correct answer.

NH means Not Here.

6. Which of these ways will make the sum?

Whole
18

Part	Part
?	?

1 + 8   8 + 9   9 + 9   NH
  ○   ○   ○   ○

Copyright © Houghton Mifflin Company. All rights reserved.

Use with text pages 567–568.

Add Three Numbers

Find the sum.

Think
Can I use a double?
Can I make a ten?

1.   8
     8
  + 1
  _____
    17

2.   6
     3
  + 3

3.   9
     1
  + 3

4.   4
     9
  + 4

5.   8
     3
  + 7

6.   2
     2
  + 7

7.   6
     4
  + 5

8.   2
     5
  + 5

9.   7
     7
  + 2

10.   1
      1
   + 8

11. $1 + 9 + 1 =$ _____

12. $2 + 2 + 2 =$ _____

13. $6 + 6 + 4 =$ _____

14. $8 + 5 + 4 =$ _____

Test Prep

Fill in the ○ for the correct answer.
NH means Not Here.

15. Which double fact can you
    use to find the sum?

        4
        6
     + 2

$2 + 2 = 4$ $4 + 4 = 8$ $6 + 6 = 12$ NH
   ○   ○   ○   ○

Use with text pages 569–570.

Name _____ Date _____

Problem Solving
Write a Number Sentence

Write a number sentence to solve.

1. There are 10 carrot plants in the first row. In the next row there are 9 carrot plants. How many carrot plants are there in all?

   _10_ (+) _9_ = _19_

Draw or write to explain.

_____ plants in all

2. Cindy picks 3 baskets of apples the first day. She picks 4 baskets the next day. She picks 1 basket the third day. How many baskets of apples does she pick?

   ____ ◯ ____ ◯ ____ = ____

_____ baskets in all

 Test Prep

Fill in the ◯ for the correct answer.
NH means Not Here.

3. Meg has 2 bags of plums. Each bag has 7 plums. Which number sentence tells how to find the total number of plums Meg has?

   ○ 2 + 7 = 9

   ○ 7 − 2 = 5

   ○ 7 + 7 = 14

   ○ NH

Use with text pages 571–572.

Use Doubles to Subtract

Add. Then subtract.

1. $1 + 1 = \underline{2}$
   $2 - 1 = \underline{1}$

2. $2 + 2 = \underline{}$
   $4 - 2 = \underline{}$

3. $3 + 3 = \underline{}$
   $6 - 3 = \underline{}$

4. $4 + 4 = \underline{}$
   $8 - 4 = \underline{}$

5. $6 + 6 = \underline{}$
   $12 - 6 = \underline{}$

6. $9 + 9 = \underline{}$
   $18 - 9 = \underline{}$

7. $8 + 8 = \underline{}$
   $16 - 8 = \underline{}$

8. $5 + 5 = \underline{}$
   $10 - 5 = \underline{}$

9. $7 + 7 = \underline{}$
   $14 - 7 = \underline{}$

10. $\begin{array}{r} 1 \\ +1 \\ \hline \end{array}$ $\begin{array}{r} 2 \\ -1 \\ \hline \end{array}$

11. $\begin{array}{r} 2 \\ +2 \\ \hline \end{array}$ $\begin{array}{r} 4 \\ -2 \\ \hline \end{array}$

12. $\begin{array}{r} 4 \\ +4 \\ \hline \end{array}$ $\begin{array}{r} 8 \\ -4 \\ \hline \end{array}$

13. $\begin{array}{r} 5 \\ +5 \\ \hline \end{array}$ $\begin{array}{r} 10 \\ -5 \\ \hline \end{array}$

14. $\begin{array}{r} 7 \\ +7 \\ \hline \end{array}$ $\begin{array}{r} 14 \\ -7 \\ \hline \end{array}$

15. $\begin{array}{r} 10 \\ +10 \\ \hline \end{array}$ $\begin{array}{r} 20 \\ -10 \\ \hline \end{array}$

Test Prep

Solve.

16. Ellen has 16 balloons.
    She gives 8 balloons to Sam.
    How many balloons does Ellen
    have now?

    _____ balloons

Draw or write to explain.

Use with text pages 581–582.

Subtract From 13 and 14

Add. Then find the difference.

1.
$$9 + 4 = 13$$

$$13 - 9 = 4$$

$$13 - 4 = 9$$

2.
$$6 + 8$$

$$14 - 6$$

$$14 - 8$$

3.
$$7 + 5$$

$$12 - 7$$

$$12 - 5$$

4.
$$5 + 8$$

$$13 - 5$$

$$13 - 8$$

5.
$$6 + 7$$

$$13 - 6$$

$$13 - 7$$

6.
$$9 + 3$$

$$12 - 9$$

$$12 - 3$$

Test Prep

Fill in the ○ for the correct answer.

NH means Not Here.

7. Look at the addition sentence.

$$7 + 6 = 13$$

Choose a related subtraction fact.

$13 - 7 = 6$ $13 - 5 = 8$ $13 - 4 = 9$ NH

○   ○   ○   ○

Use with text pages 583–584.

Subtract From 15 and 16

Add.

Then find the difference.

> Remember to use
> the addition fact to help
> you subtract.

1.
$$8 + 6 = 14$$
$$14 - 8 = 6$$
$$14 - 6 = 8$$

2.
$$9 + 6$$
$$15 - 9$$
$$15 - 6$$

3.
$$7 + 6$$
$$13 - 7$$
$$13 - 6$$

4.
$$8 + 7$$
$$15 - 7$$
$$15 - 8$$

5.
$$6 + 10$$
$$16 - 6$$
$$16 - 10$$

6.
$$7 + 9$$
$$16 - 7$$
$$16 - 9$$

Test Prep

Fill in the ○ for the correct answer.

NH means Not Here.

7. Kim has 16 pears.

She keeps 7 pears and gives away the rest.

Which tells how many pears Kim gives away?

$9 - 7$ $9 + 7$ $16 - 7$ NH
 ○ ○ ○ ○

Use with text pages 585–586.

Subtract From 17 Through 20

Subtract.

1. $\begin{array}{r} 17 \\ -\ 8 \\ \hline \end{array}$
9

2. $\begin{array}{r} 18 \\ -10 \\ \hline \end{array}$

3. $\begin{array}{r} 20 \\ -10 \\ \hline \end{array}$

4. $\begin{array}{r} 16 \\ -\ 7 \\ \hline \end{array}$

5. $\begin{array}{r} 15 \\ -\ 6 \\ \hline \end{array}$

6. $\begin{array}{r} 17 \\ -\ 9 \\ \hline \end{array}$

7. $\begin{array}{r} 16 \\ -\ 9 \\ \hline \end{array}$

8. $\begin{array}{r} 16 \\ -\ 8 \\ \hline \end{array}$

9. $\begin{array}{r} 14 \\ -\ 6 \\ \hline \end{array}$

10. $\begin{array}{r} 15 \\ -\ 5 \\ \hline \end{array}$

11. $\begin{array}{r} 15 \\ -\ 8 \\ \hline \end{array}$

12. $\begin{array}{r} 16 \\ -\ 6 \\ \hline \end{array}$

13. $\begin{array}{r} 13 \\ -\ 9 \\ \hline \end{array}$

14. $\begin{array}{r} 14 \\ -\ 9 \\ \hline \end{array}$

15. $\begin{array}{r} 17 \\ -\ 8 \\ \hline \end{array}$

Test Prep

Fill in the ○ for the correct answer.

NH means Not Here.

16. Peter has 19 marbles.

    He gives 9 marbles to Sarah.

    Which sentence tells how many

    marbles Peter has now?

$19 - 10 = 9$ ○ $19 - 9 = 10$ ○ $10 + 9 = 19$ ○   NH ○

Use with text pages 589–590.

Name _____ Date _____

Relate Addition and Subtraction

Write the missing numbers.

1. $13 - 8 =$ __5__

   $8 +$ __5__ $= 13$

2. $12 - 7 =$ ___

   $7 +$ ___ $= 12$

3. $20 - 10 =$ ___

   $10 +$ ___ $= 20$

4. $16 - 8 =$ ___

   $8 +$ ___ $= 16$

5. $14 - 8 =$ ___

   $8 +$ ___ $= 14$

6. $17 - 8 =$ ___

   $8 +$ ___ $= 17$

7. $18 - 9 =$ ___

   $9 +$ ___ $= 18$

8. $13 - 6 =$ ___

   $6 +$ ___ $= 13$

Test Prep

Fill in the ○ for the correct answer.
NH means Not Here.

13. What number do you need to complete
the addition and the subtraction sentences?

$8 +$ ___ $= 14$ $14 - 8 =$ ___

6   8   14   NH
○   ○   ○   ○

Use with text pages 591–592.

Fact Families

Complete the fact family.

1.
15	
8	7

8
+ 7
15

7
+ 8
15

15
− 7
8

15
− 8
7

2.
12	
7	5

7
+ 5

+

12
− 7

−

Test Prep

Fill in the ○ for the correct answer.

NH means Not Here.

3. Which number sentence
   completes the fact family?

$8 + 7 = 15$ $15 - 7 = 8$ $15 - 8 = 7$

$7 + 6 = 14$ $6 + 9 = 15$ $9 + 6 = 15$ NH
   ○   ○   ○   ○

Use with text pages 593–594.

Name _____ Date _____

Practice
20.7

Problem Solving
Too Much Information

Cross out the information you do not need.
Solve.

Draw or write to explain.

1. Ted sees 17 goats in a barn.
   There are 8 black and 9
   brown goats. 10 goats leave
   the barn. How many goats
   are in the barn now?

   __7__ goats

2. Reva finds 12 big stones.
   Evan finds 8 small stones.
   Reva says 8 of her stones
   are red. How many more
   stones did Reva find than Evan?

   _____ stones

Test Prep

Fill in the ○ for the correct answer.
NH means Not Here.

3. Bob bought 19 goldfish.
   10 are orange. The rest are black.
   15 are male. How many goldfish are black?

   Which information is not needed?

   ○ 10 goldfish are orange.   ○ 15 goldfish are male.

   ○ Bob bought 19 goldfish.   ○ NH

Copyright © Houghton Mifflin Company. All rights reserved.

Use with text pages 595–596.

140

Name _____ Date _____

Mental Math: Add Tens

Complete the addition sentences.

1.

$3 + 4 = \underline{7}$

$3 \text{ tens} + 4 \text{ tens} = \underline{7} \text{ tens}$

$\underline{30} + \underline{40} = \underline{70}$

2. $1 \text{ ten} + 4 \text{ tens} = \underline{\quad} \text{ tens}$

$\underline{\quad} + \underline{\quad} = \underline{\quad}$

3. $5 \text{ tens} + 3 \text{ tens} = \underline{\quad} \text{ tens}$

$\underline{\quad} + \underline{\quad} = \underline{\quad}$

4. $2 \text{ tens} + 7 \text{ tens} = \underline{\quad} \text{ tens}$

$\underline{\quad} + \underline{\quad} = \underline{\quad}$

5. $4 \text{ tens} + 5 \text{ tens} = \underline{\quad} \text{ tens}$

$\underline{\quad} + \underline{\quad} = \underline{\quad}$

Test Prep

Fill in the ○ for the correct answer.
NH means Not Here.

6. Anya has 4 groups of 10 pennies.
   How many pennies does she have?

4 pennies   10 pennies   40 pennies   NH
○   ○   ○   ○

Use with text pages 603–604.

Name _____ Date _____

Add With 2-Digit Numbers

Use Workmat 5 and ▭▭▭▭▭▭ and ▢.
Add. Write the sum.

1.
Tens	Ones
3	2
+	5
3	*7*

2.
Tens	Ones
8	2
+	7

3.
Tens	Ones
6	6
+	3

4.
Tens	Ones
2	4
+	4

5.
Tens	Ones
5	1
+	7

6.
Tens	Ones
7	7
+	2

7.
Tens	Ones
6	2
+	3

8.
Tens	Ones
4	5
+	4

Test Prep

Fill in the ○ for the correct answer.
NH means Not Here.

9. Which exercise is shown
   by these models?

Tens	Ones
5	4
+	2
○

Tens	Ones
5	0
+	6
○

Tens	Ones
5	0
+	2
○

NH
○

Use with text pages 605–606.

142

Add Two-Digit Numbers

Use Workmat 5 and ⬭⬭⬭⬭⬭ and ▫ .
Add. Write the sum.

1.
Tens	Ones
3	1
+ 1	4
4	5

2.
Tens	Ones
4	5
+ 2	2

3.
Tens	Ones
1	8
+ 4	1

4.
Tens	Ones
6	3
+ 2	5

5.
Tens	Ones
1	7
+ 6	2

6.
Tens	Ones
2	4
+ 3	3

7.
Tens	Ones
6	0
+ 1	9

8.
Tens	Ones
4	6
+ 4	3

9.
Tens	Ones
1	2
+ 7	6

10.
Tens	Ones
7	0
+ 2	7

11.
Tens	Ones
5	2
+ 3	1

12.
Tens	Ones
5	7
+ 1	1

Test Prep

Solve.

Draw or write to explain.

13. Molly plays catch for
23 minutes. Later she plays
catch for **16** minutes. How
many minutes does Molly
play catch in all ?

_____ minutes

Use with text pages 607–608.

Different Ways to Add

Choose a way to add.
Write the sum.

Think
You can use mental math.
You can use paper and pencil.
You can use tens and ones blocks.

1. $\begin{array}{r} 76 \\ +13 \\ \hline \end{array}$
2. $\begin{array}{r} 38 \\ +10 \\ \hline \end{array}$
3. $\begin{array}{r} 74 \\ +12 \\ \hline \end{array}$
4. $\begin{array}{r} 63 \\ +25 \\ \hline \end{array}$

5. $\begin{array}{r} 20 \\ +8 \\ \hline \end{array}$
6. $\begin{array}{r} 16 \\ +3 \\ \hline \end{array}$
7. $\begin{array}{r} 40 \\ +29 \\ \hline \end{array}$
8. $\begin{array}{r} 13 \\ +55 \\ \hline \end{array}$

9. $25 + 4 = $ _____

10. $30 + 10 = $ _____

11. $10 + 25 = $ _____

12. $73 + 5 = $ _____

13. $85 + 4 = $ _____

14. $15 + 60 = $ _____

Test Prep

Fill in the ○ for the correct answer.
NH means Not Here.

15. Roland keeps 32 toy cars in a box.
The box holds 35 toy cars. How
many more toy cars can Roland
put into the box before it is full?

67   35   3   NH
○   ○   ○   ○

Use with text pages 611–612.

Two-Digit Addition Practice

Write the sum.

1. $\begin{array}{r} 1\,4 \\ +\,1\,1 \\ \hline 2\,5 \end{array}$

2. $\begin{array}{r} 5\,0 \\ +\,2\,3 \\ \hline \end{array}$

3. $\begin{array}{r} 6\,0 \\ +\quad 9 \\ \hline \end{array}$

4. $\begin{array}{r} 4\,6 \\ +\,1\,3 \\ \hline \end{array}$

5. $\begin{array}{r} 7\,6 \\ +\,2\,2 \\ \hline \end{array}$

6. $\begin{array}{r} 5\,4 \\ +\,3\,2 \\ \hline \end{array}$

7. $\begin{array}{r} 2\,0 \\ +\,5\,3 \\ \hline \end{array}$

8. $\begin{array}{r} 4\,4 \\ +\,4\,3 \\ \hline \end{array}$

9. $\begin{array}{r} 1\,8 \\ +\,5\,0 \\ \hline \end{array}$

10. $\begin{array}{r} 2\,1 \\ +\,5\,8 \\ \hline \end{array}$

11. $\begin{array}{r} 8\,0 \\ +\,1\,4 \\ \hline \end{array}$

12. $\begin{array}{r} 6\,2 \\ +\,2\,3 \\ \hline \end{array}$

13. $\begin{array}{r} 2\,5 \\ +\,4\,0 \\ \hline \end{array}$

14. $\begin{array}{r} 3\,6 \\ +\,2\,1 \\ \hline \end{array}$

15. $\begin{array}{r} 5\,1 \\ +\,1\,5 \\ \hline \end{array}$

16. $\begin{array}{r} 4\,6 \\ +\,1\,1 \\ \hline \end{array}$

Test Prep

Solve.

Draw or write to explain.

17. The chidren collected
34 box tops in April. They
collected 42 box tops in May.
The children need 70 box tops
in all. Do they have enough?

Use with text pages 613–614.

Name _____ Date _____

Problem Solving: Guess and Check

Use Guess and Check to solve.

Crayon Boxes			
A	B	C	D
12	24	45	62

Draw or write to explain.

1. Sophie takes 2 boxes with 57 crayons to her friends. Which 2 boxes does she take?

box _____ and box _____

2. Leando gives away 74 crayons. Which 2 boxes does he give away?

box _____ and box _____

Test Prep

Fill in the ○ for the correct answer.
NH means Not Here.

3. José and Fredrico want 86 crayons.
   Which boxes do they want?
   Use the chart above to solve.

A and B   B and D   C and A   NH
   ○   ○   ○   ○

Use with text pages 615–616.

Subtract Tens

Complete the subtraction sentences.

1.

7 tens − 2 tens = ___5___ tens

70 − 20 = 50

2. 9 tens − 6 tens = _____ tens

90 − 60 = _____

3. 8 tens − 4 tens = _____ tens

80 − 40 = _____

4. 3 tens − 2 tens = _____ ten

30 − 20 = _____

Test Prep

5. There are 50 children in a drawing class. There are 30 children in a pottery class. How many more children are in the drawing class?

Draw or write to explain.

_____ more children

Use with text pages 625–626.

Name _____ Date _____

Subtract With Two-Digit Numbers

Use Workmat 5 with ▭▭▭▭ and ▱.
Subtract. Write the difference.

1.
Tens	Ones
1	7
−	5
1	2

2.
Tens	Ones
2	6
−	3

3.
Tens	Ones
2	9
−	5

4.
Tens	Ones
3	8
−	4

5.
Tens	Ones
3	5
−	4

6.
Tens	Ones
4	6
−	5

7.
Tens	Ones
4	9
−	7

8.
Tens	Ones
5	7
−	3

9.
Tens	Ones
6	8
−	6

10.
Tens	Ones
7	4
−	2

11.
Tens	Ones
8	9
−	6

12.
Tens	Ones
9	9
−	7

Test Prep

13. There are 37 children in the school band. 4 children play the tuba. How many children play other instruments in the school band?

Draw or write to explain.

_____ children

Use with text pages 627–628.

Name _____ Date _____

Subtract Two-Digit Numbers

Use Workmat 5 with ⬚⬚⬚⬚⬚ and ▢. Subtract.
Write the difference.

1.
Tens	Ones
5	6
− 2	3
3	3

2.
Tens	Ones
4	7
− 2	2

3.
Tens	Ones
4	4
− 1	3

4.
Tens	Ones
6	9
− 4	8

5.
Tens	Ones
5	3
− 4	1

6.
Tens	Ones
7	8
− 1	7

7.
Tens	Ones
7	7
− 3	6

8.
Tens	Ones
6	4
− 2	2

9.
Tens	Ones
8	8
− 3	6

10.
Tens	Ones
9	6
− 3	1

11.
Tens	Ones
8	3
− 4	2

12.
Tens	Ones
9	8
− 2	2

Test Prep

Fill in the ○ for the correct answer.
NH means Not Here.

13. A box has 27 apples and 15 pears.
How many more apples than pears
are in the box?

4 ○   32 ○   13 ○   12 ○   NH ○

Use with text pages 629–630.

Different Ways to Subtract

Choose a way to subtract.
Write the difference.

I can use mental math.
I can use paper and pencil.
I can use tens and ones blocks.

Tens	Ones
7	4
− 3	1
4	3

1.

2.

Tens	Ones
3	8
−	7

3.

Tens	Ones
9	0
− 7	0

4.

Tens	Ones
5	4
−	3

5. $98 - 67$

6. $65 - 2$

7. $78 - 26$

8. $66 - 30$

9. $70 - 50$

10. $76 - 12$

11. $99 - 68$

12. $87 - 3$

13. $80 - 30 =$ _____

14. $42 - 2 =$ _____

15. $46 - 6 =$ _____

16. $73 - 3 =$ _____

Test Prep

17. Joel finds 10 large stones and 25 small stones. He gives 4 stones to his sister. How many stones does he have now? _____ stones

Draw or write to explain.

Use with text pages 631–632.

Name _____ Date _____

Two-Digit Subtraction Practice

Write the difference.

1. 21
   -11
   ____
    10

2. 40
   -30
   ____

3. 58
   -32
   ____

4. 74
   -12
   ____

5. 96
   - 4
   ____

6. 64
   - 3
   ____

7. 95
   -24
   ____

8. 55
   -33
   ____

9. 96
   -43
   ____

10. 26
    -14
    ____

11. 74
    -42
    ____

12. 65
    -41
    ____

13. 86
    -35
    ____

14. 76
    - 5
    ____

15. 49
    - 5
    ____

16. 36
    -23
    ____

17. 54
    -33
    ____

18. 90
    -20
    ____

19. 79
    -13
    ____

20. 87
    -45
    ____

Test Prep

Fill in the ○ for the correct answer.

NH means Not Here.

21. Zack has 33 stickers. His sister
    Kayla has 21 stickers. How many
    more stickers does Zack
    have than Kayla?

    12   14   54   NH
    ○   ○   ○   ○

Use with text pages 635–636.

Check Subtraction

Subtract. Check by adding.

1. 78
   – 6
   ――――
    72   + 78

2. 60
   – 10
   ――――   +

3. 64
   – 23
   ――――   +

4. 58
   – 30
   ――――   +

Test Prep

Fill in the ○ for the correct answer.

NH means Not Here.

5. How many fewer children like grapes than apples?

Best Fruit Votes	Total
Apples	38
Grapes	28
Oranges	20

$38 - 20 = 18$ $38 - 28 = 10$ $28 - 20 = 8$ NH
     ○   ○   ○   ○

Use with text pages 637–638.

Name _____ Date _____

Problem Solving: Choose the Operation

Add or subtract to solve.
Write the number sentence.

1. Sarah has 15 silver balloons and 28 blue balloons. How many more blue balloons are there?

28
○ − 15
‾‾‾‾‾
13

___13___ more blue balloons

2. Jake has 32 baseball cards. Betty has 35 baseball cards. How many baseball cards do they have in all?

[ ]
○ [ ]
‾‾‾‾
[ ]

_____ baseball cards in all

3. On Saturday Karen takes 14 pictures. On Sunday she takes 21 pictures. How many pictures does she take on both days?

[ ]
○ [ ]
‾‾‾‾
[ ]

_____ pictures

Test Prep

4. Larry sees 25 birds at the park. Kendra sees 37 birds. How many more birds does Kendra see?

[ ]
○ [ ]
‾‾‾‾
[ ]

_____ more birds

Use with text pages 639–642.